D1229485

GILL'S IRISH LIVES

JAMES CRAIG
LORD CRAIGAVON

PATRICK BUCKLAND

GILL AND MACMILLAN

First published 1980 by
Gill and Macmillan Ltd
15/17 Eden Quay
Dublin 1
with associated companies in
London, New York, Delhi, Hong Kong,
Johannesburg, Lagos, Melbourne,
Singapore, Tokyo

0 7171 0984 4 (paperback)

0 7171 1078 8 (hardback)

available in this series:
Michael Collins (Leon O'Broin)
Sean O'Casey (Hugh Hunt)
C. S. Parnell (Paul Bew)
James Craig (Patrick Buckland)
James Joyce (Peter Costello)
Eamon de Valera (T. Ryle Dwyer)

in preparation:
George Bernard Shaw (Kenneth Richards)
W. T. Cosgrave (Maurice Manning)
Daniel O'Connell (Kevin B. Nowlan)
Theobald Wolfe Tone (Henry Boylan)
Edward Carson (A. T. Q. Stewart)
Sean Lemass (Brian Farrell)
Arthur Griffith (Calton Younger)

Origination by Healyset, Dublin
Printed in Great Britain by
Redwood Burn Ltd.
Trowbridge & Esher

Contents

Acknowledgments

Yet again I wish to thank the Director of the Public Record Office of Northern Ireland for permission to use and reproduce extracts from the various official and non-official papers deposited in the office; his staff for their unstinting help; and Mr Colm Croker, my editor, for his constructive interest and pertinent suggestions; and Miss Yvonne Jones both for encouragement in writing and for generous assistance in proof-reading.

Acknowledgmen

Abbreviations

IRA   Irish Republican Army
PR   Proportional representation
RUC   Royal Ulster Constabulary
UPA   Ulster Protestant Association
UUC   Ulster Unionist Council
UVF   Ulster Volunteer Force

Note on terminology

A small initial letter has been used when referring to general matters connected with the needs and demands of Irish nationality, but an initial capital has been used for 'Nationalist' to indentify the heirs of the old Irish Parliamentary Party in Northern Ireland. Since the government in London was often described by Ulster Unionists as the 'imperial government', this practice has been adopted to distinguish the London government, its ministers and civil servants from other governments and their ministers and officials. Finally, although Craig was created Viscount Craigavon of Stormont in 1927, he has for convenience been referred to throughout by his surname.

Introduction

His countrymen believed . . . that James Craig was, under God, chosen to perform a task that must have baffled, if not defeated, any other person. . . . James Craig, bone of their bone, and flesh of their flesh, alien to them neither in belief nor in birth, achieved what no other man could have achieved. Against that rock, the gates of the Eirean hell could not prevail.[1]

That his official biographer had to resort to such heroic rhetoric to describe James Craig and his relations with his Ulster Unionist supporters serves only to underline that Craig's hold over the majority of people in Northern Ireland was due almost entirely to his unexceptional qualities. He was the embodiment of ordinariness. Big, bluff, stolid and kindly-looking with a large, red, craggy face, his appearance reflected much of his character — humane, unimaginative, a man who could be relied upon to do a competent job. Had he been born in any part of the United Kingdom other than Ireland, he would probably have had a moderately successful political career, fitting in well with those grey men who dominated British politics in the inter-war years.

But Craig had not been born in Britain. Instead he had been born in the north of Ireland in 1871, the son of a Presbyterian whiskey millionaire who bought land for himself and status for his children. In some

respects Craig did as other young men of his back‐
[2] ground in the United Kingdom did. He made a good marriage; he volunteered to fight and served with dis‐ tinction in the South African War; and he entered parliament at Westminister and eventually held government office. Yet the fact that he had been born an Ulster Protestant enabled him to develop his one outstanding talent — the power of organisation, which gave this ordinary man an extraordinary career as the architect of the partition of Ireland. He master‐ minded Ulster Unionist resistance to the Third Home Rule Bill; he constructed the new region of Northern Ireland; and he presided over its early years in which was established a pattern of government and politics that eventually ended in violence.

1
Backbencher

'I used to murmur because I had no shoes, until I met a man who had no feet.'[1] It is difficult to dislike a man such as James Craig, 1st Viscount Craigavon, who could quote this Arab proverb. It summed up Craig's temperament and attitude to life: a stolid calmness and acceptance which was not belied by his solid, Colonel Blimp-like appearance — his heavy build and thick-set features. Such qualities, though admirable, would have made him an extremely difficult subject for a biography had it not been for his involvement after 1911 in Ulster Unionists' resistance to Home Rule. Until then Craig's life was conventional and routine. He was born with no sense of mission, was distinguished by no great personal or intellectual gifts, and found difficulty in settling down to a job.

1

He was born on 8 January 1871 in Co. Down, just outside Belfast, to a Presbyterian family that had little claim to notice but its money and the eccentricity of his father. His father, also James Craig, was a self-made whiskey millionaire, whose Scottish ancestors had settled in Ulster probably in the seventeenth century but had lived in Co. Down since the early eighteenth century. A man of ambition, energy, determination, industry and high powers of organisation, Craig's father had rejected the routine life of the

Civil Service and had become a flour-miller's clerk,
[4] then a clerk in a linen-bleaching works, and then
a clerk in Dunville's Distillery, Belfast. This last move
made both him and the firm. He was twenty-eight
and poor when he joined Dunville's which was in
difficulties in 1856, but within twenty years he was
a millionaire and the firm was world-renowned.
Although well-known as a 'character', he was scarcely
a likeable man, being close with money and usually
acting with scant regard for the feelings of others.
He 'did what he wanted to do. He went directly to his
object, and did not wait to hear what was the cus-
tomary way.'[2]

Craig's mother, Eleanor Gilmore, was of different
mettle. Descended from a Scottish family which had
settled in Ulster early in the eighteenth century, she
was an attractive, good-natured woman with graceful
and gentle manners, and was remembered by her
friends for her placid, calm and unobtrusive character
and her implusive generosity. So likeable was she that
her daughters-in-law used to complain that they did
not see enough of her! She married her husband in
1858, after a swift and impetuous courtship, when
she was twenty-three and he thirty. They became
parents of eight sons and one daughter, Craig being
the seventh child and sixth son.

Craig spent his childhood in the countryside and
seaside of Co. Down, where his father had bought
property. Shortly after his birth the family moved
to a new house, Craigavon, architecturally unattractive
but standing in lovely curving meadows, close to the
city of Belfast but well into the country and only a
little distance from the Lough. In addition, there was
a holiday home, Tyrella, bordered by two miles of
sandy beaches and 'confronting the Irish Sea where it
rolls into Dundrum Bay, a water full of sandbanks
and black, forbidding rocks'.[3] Tyrella itself was much

more than a holiday home: it was a demense standing in a part of Co. Down, the ancient Kingdom of [5] Mourne, which was almost musty with myth and legend. Indeed, the memories left by Tyrella on the young Craig's mind were so deep and tender that when his eldest brother, Clarence, sold it, he felt so embittered that he could never bring himself to enter its grounds again.

Home life was comfortable but simple and unaffected. His father had no political ambitions and maintained the routine of a businessman, and Craig's position in the family was fortunate. Coming in the second half, he was subject to the discipline of elder brothers, but arrived just long enough after the birth of his only sister to benefit from her affection, care and companionship, and just soon enough before the birth of his two younger brothers to be able to exercise some authority over them. Although strict to the point of austerity when they became adult, Craig's father was indulgent in their childhood, while his mother quietly corrected the faults that indulgence encouraged. Craig had, in fact, a happy and uneventful childhood. He was no infant prodigy but 'merely a happy lad, larking about Craigavon and Tyrella, running to market with hinds, following the ploughman, rowing a boat and going, but not unwillingly, to school'.[4]

His schooling did not cut him off from his Ulster roots. He attended a preparatory school, some three miles from Craigavon, run by a Presbyterian minister in a room underneath his church, and in 1882 was sent to Merchiston Castle School, Edinburgh, a Church of Scotland public school. He thus avoided, much to the relief of his earlier biographers, exposure to the effects of the English public school system and retained 'an Ulster mind and an Ulster accent'.[5] His life at Merchiston was unspectacular. He was fond of games,

especially football, without being good at them: 'a
[6] good dribbler, but short of pace'.[6] He became a pre-
fect and once lectured on Ireland to the Literary and
Debating Society, but he did not distinguish himself
by scholarship. If anything, he was distinguished by
his character, his headmaster once publicly stating:
'James Craig would never do a dishonourable thing.'[7]

2

It was after leaving school at the age of seventeen that
Craig's problems began. His father expected his sons
to earn a living. Two sons joined their father in the
distillery, one became a railway engineer, one an
architect, one an electrical and general engineer, and
another a solicitor. None went to university, and Craig
himself was first put into a firm of general agents and
brokers in Belfast, where he learned the elements of
office work by addressing envelopes, licking stamps
and carrying the mail to the post office. After thirty
months of such servitude his father sent him to London to join a stockbroking firm, and after a two-
year apprenticeship there he returned to Ulster to
open his own stockbroking firm, Craigs & Co., Belfast.

A founder-member of the Belfast Stock Exchange,
he became a successful broker, but his heart and soul
were not in the buying and selling of shares. In fact
he was more interested in yachting than in stockbroking, and he enjoyed racing boats on the Belfast
and Strangford Loughs, where, it was said, he knew
every current, rock and shoal. He became an Associate
of the Institute of Naval Architects and a member of
the Yacht-Racing Association and the Royal Ulster
Yacht Club, whom in 1901 he represented in the
United States in connection with the America Cup
Race. His career at sea was, however, largely curtailed

by colour-blindness, when he discovered that he could not distinguish red from green — which also [7] meant that he could hardly distinguish orange from green!

He was so uninvolved in his profession that he eagerly seized the chance to enlist when the South African War broke out late in 1899 between the British Empire and the small Boer Republic of the Transvaal. Returning to an earlier ambition to join the army, he volunteered for service and on 17 January 1900 took a commission in the 3rd (Militia) Battalion of the Royal Irish Rifles, ceasing formally to be a member of the Belfast Stock Exchange on 6 March following. The war was, as far as the British were concerned, an incompetently managed affair, and Craig, who was seconded, as lieutenant and then as captain, to the 6th Company of the Imperial Yeomanry, found himself increasingly angry at the way in which he and his men suffered from the ineptitude and arrogance of senior regular army officers. He himself, however, proved a good and popular officer and a true soldier. Taken prisoner by the Boers, he elected to march with his men instead of riding with the other officers to the prison camp two hundred miles away.

His imprisonment was short-lived. A splinter from an exploding gun, which had earlier burst his eardrum, became very painful, and his captors, unable to help, chivalrously put him across the border into Portuguese territory. On his recovery, he became Deputy Assistant Director of the Imperial Military Railways, and it was in this capacity that he displayed those remarkable powers of organisation and attention to detail which later stood the Ulster Unionist movement in such good stead. To prepare himself for the post, he bought a model railway on which he practised signalling and worked out the details of the block system. His labour on the single track was so well done that columns never had to wait long for a train.

His part in the South African War ended in June 1901, when he was invalided home suffering from dysentery. By the time he returned to South Africa, this time in command of D Squadron of the 29th Battalion of the Imperial Yeomanry, the war was almost over, and a crucial period in Craig's life came to an end. Politically he had developed, for the war had given him a heightened awareness of the Empire and a pride in Ulster's place in it. Personally, too, the foundations of his character were revealed to others and himself: his friendliness, his sense of responsibility for those under his command, his steadfastness and independence, and his extraordinary administrative ability. Indeed, his qualities, particularly his sense of order and neatness, surprised his senior officers. Such a heavy-looking man might have been expected to wield a pen as if it were a broadsword, but he had a writing hand that a medieval monk, illuminating missals, might have envied. It was clear and regular and well shaped, deviating not at all from a line so straight that it might have been rigidly ruled. 'An extraordinary man,' said the company paymaster. 'His accounts all kept in his own handwriting, balance to a penny after a year and a half of active service!'[8]

3

It was the death of his father rather than the impact of his experiences in the South African War which enabled Craig to develop a new life when the war ended. His father had died a wealthy man on 28 April 1900, leaving Craig a legacy of £100,000. Craig declined the opportunity to serve in the regular army, although he did not retire from the militia until July 1908. Nor was he interested in reopening his stockbroking business. Eventually he decided to pursue a career in politics.

He had shown some mild interest in politics before the South African War, when he had briefly acted as honorary secretary of the Belfast Conservative Association, but his interest was stimulated by the return to Westminster of his elder brother, Charles Curtis Craig, as the Unionist MP for South Antrim in a by-election on 6 February 1903. There was never any doubt which of Ireland's political parties Craig would stand for. He had been brought up as a matter of course a supporter of the Irish Unionist movement, which since the 1880s had been combating the demand of the nationalist Irish Parliamentary Party for Home Rule, and which had of late also been fighting a Liberal or Russellite party especially interested in the rights of farmers. In March 1903 he was unexpectedly selected against strong local rivals as Unionist candidate to fill a sudden vacancy in North Fermanagh. His selection owed little to his political acumen and much to the fact that he was the only prospective Unionist candidate willing and able to finance the campaign himself without calling on the funds of the impoverished local association. Although he was narrowly defeated by a Russellite, the hard-fought contest was a useful training for his candidature in his native constituency of East Down. On 11 November 1903 he was formally adopted as the Unionist opponent to the sitting Russellite member, a well-connected local man, and nursed the constituency so effectively that in the general election of January 1906, at the age of thirty-five, he won the seat with a majority of 607. Henceforth it was his seat, which he held in the two general elections of 1910 with increased majorities.*

Craig's electioneering was distinguished not by any

*He continued to sit for East Down until the general election of 1918, when, following an increase in the number of Co. Down constituencies, he was returned with a majority of 9,932 for Mid-Down, from which he resigned in 1921.

originality or brilliance of political ideas but by the
[10] courtesy with which he treated his opponents and by
the vigour of his campaigning by motor-bike or car.
Indeed, farmers told each other tales of how they had
seen him tearing round and round the country lanes
on a motor-cycle until its petrol had given out, because
he had learned how to start it but had forgotten how
to stop it! His main plank was opposition to Home
Rule and the maintenance of the legislative Union
between Great Britain and Ireland. In addition, he
pragmatically and eclectically included in his election
programme most of the notions then exciting the
interest of politicians, such as non-sectarian education,
tariff reform, and even votes for women; but he also
liked to stress, as was only politic in a farming constituency, his agricultural background and the fact
that he had been farming for many years in Co. Down.

Craig's political ambitions were fostered rather
than hindered by his marriage on 22 March 1905 to
Cecil Mary Nowell Dering Tupper, daughter of Daniel
(later Sir Daniel) Tupper, Assistant Comptroller of
the Lord Chamberlain's Department of the King's
Household. Craig had met her only six months previously at a shooting party in Co. Tyrone, but, like
his father's wooing, Craig's was impetuous and well
founded. The marriage was successful. There were
three children, twin boys (born on 2 March 1906) and
a girl (born on 20 August 1907), and Craig's wife,
herself intensely interested in politics, encouraged his
career, particularly by adapting her English and
Anglican ways to the moods and customs of Noncon-
formist Ulster.

The year 1906 was not the best time to enter parliament as a Unionist, for the Conservative and Unionist
Party was in disarray at Westminster. The Liberals
had won a landslide victory in the general election
and continued to hold office, admittedly with reduced

majorities, after the two general elections of 1910. Conservatives and Unionists were thus condemned to [11] years of opposition and internal wrangling, but those Unionist MPs returned for Ireland (nineteen, mainly Ulstermen, in 1906) were less affected and demoralised.

The Irish Unionist MPs at Westminster had their own organisation and had a more clearly defined objective than Unionists in Britain. Opposition to Home Rule was their overriding concern, and since the Liberal Party was the party of Home Rule, the Irish Unionist Party adopted a vigorous campaign against the Irish administration. There was little prospect of a fully-fledged Home Rule Bill being introduced in the 1906 parliament, but the Liberal administration still laid itself open to Unionist attack on account of its general sympathy towards Irish Nationalists and its intention to introduce, as it did abortively in 1907, a mild measure of devolution. The honorary secretary of the Irish Unionist Party, John (later Sir John) B. Lonsdale, the MP for Mid-Armagh, actually established a record in 1908 by addressing to ministers no fewer than 370 questions, mainly on the subject of lawlessness in Ireland. A disgruntled Augustine Birrell, the Chief Secretary for Ireland, was not surprisingly moved to liken his questioners to 'carrion crows', asking questions 'for the sole purpose of maligning and misrepresenting their native country'.[9] The campaign may have had only a marginal influence on the Liberals' Irish policy, but it was much appreciated by the Opposition at large in their search for any issue on which to attack the government.

As one of the band of Irish Unionist MPs, Craig entered fully and skilfully into this campaign against the Irish administration, much to the surprise of Nationalists, who had expected him to be slow on the uptake. Soon they began to bait him and his equally

pertinacious and swift brother, Charles. Indeed,
[12] Craig's imperturbable manner and his ability to talk
at length, but in order, on any subject were quickly
exploited by the Opposition whips. He held the House
while absent members were hurriedly brought back to
the chamber, or he simply wasted the government's
time to delay legislation.

Yet Craig also remained his own man, taking an
especial interest in two matters. One was the state of
the British army, particularly the role of volunteers.
His first parliamentary question, on 28 February
1906, asked the Secretary of State for War if he was
aware of the inconvenience and loss of civilian pay
caused to men of the militia battalions of the Royal
Irish Rifles by their having to assemble for training in
the middle of one week and to disband in the middle
of another. His maiden speech occured a week later,
on 8 March, on the army estimates, not to criticise
the War Secretary but to underline the importance of
volunteers in time of war and to point out the mis-
management and discourtesy which had characterised
their treatment during the South African War.

Education was the other question in which Craig
took a persisent interest. His first parliamentary committee was in connection with the Education (Provision of Meals) Bill, 1906, which provided for the
feeding of necessitous schoolchildren, but it was the
state of education in Ireland that most concerned him.
Suspicious of the influence of the Catholic Church,
he preached the need for non-sectarian education at
all levels, but his main preoccupation was that in
respect of teachers' salaries and the heating and clean-
ing of schools Ireland lagged behind Britain. His campaign to improve the financial provision for Irish
education began on 12 December 1906, and in the
following June he introduced for the first time, under
the ten minutes rule, an Irish National Schools (Heat-

ing and Cleansing) Bill. 'The measure', he remarked, 'is entirely non-party and undenominational, and I trust that it will be considered as uncontroversial.'[10] His proposals were also relatively inexpensive, but the bill was talked out in 1907 and made no progress when Craig re-presented it annually for the next few years. Almost any other man would have been discouraged by these failures and rebuffs, but not Craig. And far from trying the patience of the House, his perseverance won admiration, even drawing by 1911 a compliment from the much-harried Birrell. [13]

Indeed, by the time his first parliament was drawing to a close Craig had established a reputation as a useful and promising backbencher. His renown in Ulster was spreading, and on 26 January 1909 the *Northern Whig*, one of Ulster's leading daily newspapers, devoted its first leading article to Craig's evidence before a Royal Commission on Electoral Reform, in which he stressed the gross inequalities in Irish representation at Westminster and argued against proportional representation (PR). In Britain, too, his good temper, his persistent attempts to understand issues, and his passion for exactitude won the ear and liking of the House.

He was not an outstanding orator, but he had a sincerity of utterance, an exactness of statement and a penchant for reasoned argument that were extraordinarily effective. His style was clear, and his Ulster accent attractive. His words might have lacked colour and passion, but they did not lack force. 'A man whose face had been smacked by Craig was not left with the impression that his back had been stroked. . . . But he knew also that it had been smacked without prejudice or venom.'[11] These were the qualities that attracted attention and affection. As 'Toby, MP' commented in *Punch* in 1909,

This tall, broad-shouldered, florid-faced stonewaller is at once the delight and the despair of the House of Commons. . . . The activities of the honourable and gallant member were revealed in the heavy wad of amendments to the Budget Bill. Scores of motions in the Captain's name were down on the paper. He and his brother drafted hundreds of amendments to the Irish Land Bill. . . . Taunts are flung at him across the gangway by the Nationalists. No matter. The brogue-tongued Captain plods along, swamping Ministerial time and patience by the dreary drip of words. He serves his purpose — and his party. You seldom catch the Captain nodding. He is never out of order in the eyes of the Chairman. He will sit up all night in the House of Commons, turn up again at half-past eleven in the morning, make twenty speeches in Grand Committee, bolt down a light lunch, and, fresh as paint, walk into the popular Chamber in the afternoon for another long fight over the Bill of the moment.[12]

It was a pleasant tribute, but not one which set Craig glowingly apart from other rising and conventional parliamentarians. It certainly provided no hint of the dominant and scarcely constitutional role he was shortly to assume.

2
Rebel

The conventionality of Craig's political life was abruptly shattered by the onset of the crisis over the Third Home Rule Bill, 1912—14. Then Craig became a leader of the King's rebels as Ulster Unionists orga- nised themselves to defy the imperial parliament and resist the imposition of Home Rule in their province. Craig did not create the Ulster Unionist movement, and he was content to allow Sir Edward Carson to present its public face, but it was Craig who master- minded the campaign against the Third Home Rule Bill, thus giving direction to Ulster Unionism and sub- stance to Carson's defiant rhetoric, and promoting the partition of Ireland.

1

The campaign against the Third Home Rule Bill, which turned Craig from a loyal backbencher into a rebel leader, was the product of a political movement whose roots went back to the seventeenth century but whose immediate origins lay in William Ewart Gladstone's conversion to Home Rule in face of the rise of the Irish Home Rule movement under Charles Stewart Parnell. An organised and coherent Unionist counter-movement emerged among Ulster Protestants in the mid-1880s, when, in an effort to pacify Ireland and yet maintain the integrity of the British Empire, Gladstone, then Prime Minister and leader of the

Liberal Party, introduced the First Home Rule Bill. It
[16] was a mild proposal, dissolving the parliamentary
Union which had existed between Ireland and Great
Britain since 1800 and establishing an Irish parliament with limited powers. Nevertheless, the reaction
in Ulster was immediate and fierce. Liberals and
Conservatives among Ulster's Protestants sank their
political differences in a newly founded movement
dedicated to maintaining the Union. Landowners and
tenant farmers, businessmen, artisans and labourers,
all combined in a movement which cut across class
barriers and operated determinedly on two fronts —
in Ulster and in Britain. Ulster Unionists were prepared to stand on their own and resist by force of
arms if necessary the authority of a Dublin parliament, but in the first instance they preferred to fore-
stall Home Rule by persuading the British parliament
and electorate of the folly of weakening the Union
and convincing them of the justice of their objections
to Home Rule. This was the political climate in which
Craig had matured, and he readily identified with the
Ulster Unionist case for the Union.

Ulster Unionists professed themselves content with
the status quo under the Union. They enjoyed being
part of the Protestant majority of the United Kingdom and believed that Ireland, particularly the North-
East, had prospered under the Union. Most obviously,
industry had flourished in the North-East, where Belfast had established itself as the world's major linen
centre and Harland & Wolff were producing by the
early twentieth century the largest ships in the world,
including the ill-fated *Titanic*. Moreover, Ulster
Unionists were convinced that an Irish parliament
would be dominated by lower-class Catholics and
would be at the mercy of priests and agitators.
Such a prospect appalled and terrified them, for they
did not trust an Irish parliament so constituted to

deal fairly with them. Home Rule, they predicted, would result in the abrogation of civil and religious liberty and in economic and social chaos.

Such objections to Home Rule sprang from the tensions produced by the peculiar evolution of society in Ulster. Ulster was different from the rest of Ireland. History, religion and economic development not only erected barriers to understanding between Ulster Protestants and Unionists and Irish Catholics and nationalists, but also created a sense of solidarity among the former.

History divided Irishmen and gave Ulster Protestants a mythology of suspicion and hatred. Protestants had first arrived in Ulster from Britain in any strength at the beginning of the seventeenth century, as part of the English plan to subdue the recently conquered province. They had hardly been welcomed by the Gaelic and Catholic host community, deprived of its traditions and often its land. Whereas the Gaelic Irish resented and remembered the foreign occupation, Ulster Protestants long recalled with horror attempts to massacre and expel them. Time had not softened these historic differences, which were reinforced in the late nineteenth century by the Gaelic revival, as the Gaelic Athletic Association and the Gaelic League sought to emphasise the uniqueness of the Gaelic Irish — indeed, to de-anglicise Ireland.

Religion was another divisive factor. Most of Ireland was Catholic, but parts of Ulster were overwhelmingly Protestant. What is more, the predominant trends in Ulster Protestantism and Irish Catholicism were mutually antagonistic. Since the 1850s Irish Catholicism had had a strong Ultramontane streak, and from the 1880s it had experienced a new access of enthusiasm and missionary zeal, even developing a fundamental hostility towards the North. By contrast, Ulster Protestantism, the dominant strain in which was Presbyterianism, emphasised the principle [18] of salvation by grace alone and regarded the Bible as the Word of God and not merely a book about Him. Evangelical fundamentalists thus abhorred Roman Catholicism as illiberal, since the Catholic Church interfered with man's direct relationship with God. 'Popery is something more than a religious system.' claimed Ulster Protestants. 'It is a political system also. It is a religio-political system for the enslavement of the body and soul of man.'[1]

Such suspicion of Catholicism was institutionalised not only in the Protestant churches but also in the controversial Orange Order. Originating in the rural tensions of North Armagh in the 1790s, the Order had quickly become an integral part of the social and political life of Ulster and by the twentieth century embraced some two-thirds of adult male Protestants. Dedicated to maintaining the Protestant religion and the Protestant ascendancy, it gave colour and cohesion to Protestantism and Unionism in the North, both through its evocative pageantry and by acting as a link between different sections of society, since all Protestants could enter the Order on the same basis of equality.

The industrial development of the North-East also helped to explain the existence and nature of the Ulster Unionist movement. The North-East was the only part of Ireland to industrialise in the nineteenth century, and the most obvious effect was the separation of Ulster from agricultural Ireland. The North-East relied mainly on Britain and abroad for markets and materials and had more in common with Clydeside and Merseyside than with the rest of Ireland. Less obviously, but equally importantly, the nature of industrialisation helped to produce cohesion among Ulster Protestants. In particular, the Protestant working classes were willing to accept the political leadership of their employers in order to maintain full employment.

The distinctive development of Ulster engendered in Protestants there a sense of community and common interest and enabled them to combine in a mass movement which crossed class barriers but was directed by the 'upper classes'. Irishmen were, in fact, divided before partition. There may be room for debate as to how far Ulster Unionists constituted a separate nation. They themselves had only a very hazy sense of nationality. They neither felt themselves truly British, which is why they identified so strongly with the Empire instead of Britain the nation state, nor could they reject their Irishness. As one Ulster Unionist remarked in 1914, 'If in one sense, Ulstermen are Irishmen first and Britishers afterwards, in another sense they are Ulstermen first and Irishmen afterwards.'[2] Yet, however uncertain they may have been of their national identity, Ulster Unionists were absolutely certain that they were different from the Catholic majority of Ireland. If there were not two nations, there certainly were, according to one leader, two Irelands — one 'loyal', the other 'disloyal'. The latter sought 'by intimidation, by murder, by threats of revolt and separation . . . to extort by force from English fear that which England's reason refuses to concede', while 'loyal Ireland', Unionist Ireland, strove 'for their country's welfare by every lawful method within the lines of the Constitution of the Empire'.[3]

Such were the ideas and circumstances which moulded Craig's political thinking. As a Presbyterian he was a member of Ulster's largest and most uncompromising Protestant denomination. He was also, as were most leading Ulster Unionists, a member of the Orange Order. Indeed, as Grand Master of the Co. Down lodge he seemed so closely identified with the Order that he once told the Northern Ireland House of Commons that 'I am an Orangeman first and a [20] politician and Member of this Parliament afterwards.'[4] This controversial and widely quoted remark, made in the heat of debate, did less than justice to Craig. He was no bigot and never personally endorsed the often extreme sentiments and claims of the Order. Nevertheless, the fact that he made the remark at all underlined not only the political influence the Order could exercise but also the extent to which Craig identified with and acted within the Protestant traditions of Ulster. He might have been more tolerant and goodnatured than most Ulster Protestants and Unionists, but he had almost unthinkingly absorbed all their conventional notions and had come to share their fears and prejudices.

Thus he had the general Ulster Protestant distrust of the Catholic Church. 'At every stage in life from the cradle to the grave', he once wrote, 'the Roman Catholic Church intervenes, exhorting and commanding her adherents to have no intercourse with Protestants. . . . Ireland was the most priest-ridden country in the world.' Nor was he any more complimentary about Irish nationalists. Ireland's substantial economic progress under the Union would have been much greater, he asserted, 'if the people had been encouraged in industry and thrift instead of being turned into beggars and mendicants at the instance of professional agitators.' In such circumstances, he maintained, Home Rule would 'at least be a risk for Ulster, and why should Ulster be asked to place in jeopardy the position she has manfully won for herself by industry and enterprise, by patience and perseverance?'[5]

2

Craig brought to Ulster Unionism nothing in the way of ideas and ideology, but he had much to offer at a more practical level to help Ulster Unionists over-come the many problems they encountered in their fight against Home Rule. Although their movement was firmly rooted in the history and development of the province, they were beset by difficulties both at home and in Britain. In Ulster, class and political divisions were often in danger of undermining cohe-sion, while the success of their appeal to Britain to maintain the Union was by no means guaranteed. The Protestantism and imperialism of Ulster did strike a response among Protestants and imperialists in Britain, especially among members of the Conservative and Unionist Party, but the success of the Ulster Unionists' appeal was often jeopardised by their extremism, real or imagined, particularly the participation of some of them in recurrent sectarian rioting, and by the tact-lessness of their politicians. Such problems of sus-taining a disciplined interest in Unionism in Ulster and convincing the British of their just determination not to have Home Rule had been evident but not pressing at the time of the first two Home Rule Bills in 1886 and 1893. On these occasions Ulster Unionist determination and cohesion had not been fully put to the test, for a good deal of strategically placed opposition in Britain to the break-up of the Union had ensured that the First Home Rule Bill was quickly rejected by the House of Commons and its successor by the House of Lords. The Third Home Rule Bill, however, provided not only a sterner challenge to Ulster Unionists but also a personal test and oppor-tunity for Craig as one of their leading parliamentary representatives.

Expected since the Liberals' confirmation in power in December 1910, the Third Home Rule Bill was finally introduced into the Commons at West-minster on 11 April 1912. Like the two previous Home Rule Bills, it was introduced by a Liberal government, this time headed by Herbert Henry Asquith, [22] dependent on Irish Nationalist votes for a majority in the Commons. Like the other two bills, it offered Ireland only a limited form of Home Rule within the British Empire. However, unlike the controversies surrounding the first two bills, that over the third promised to be protracted, and it was probable that the new bill would become law. Not only had electoral opinion in Britain lost much of its horror of Home Rule since the 1880s, but the powers of the House of Lords had since been clipped. The Parliament Act, 1911, had abolished the absolute veto, which had allowed the Lords to kill the Second Home Rule Bill, but had left them with a suspensory veto, the power of delaying a measure for two years. Thus, although the Liberal—Nationalist majority in the Commons virtually ensured that the bill would become law, the overwhelming Unionist majority in the Lords meant that, unless a compromise were effected, the bill would not reach the statute book until the summer of 1914. Such a prolonged crisis heightened the problems which had long faced Ulster Unionism.

Admittedly, changes in the Conservative and Unionist Party in Britain did ease Ulster Unionists' relations with the Opposition. In November 1911 Arthur James Balfour, who together with his advisers was unsympathetic to 'noisy Irish Protestants',[6] was replaced as leader by Andrew Bonar Law, a Scots-Canadian Presbyterian of Ulster descent who claimed to care about only two things in politics — tariff reform and Ulster. Moreover, the party at large, frustrated at continued exclusion from power and incensed at the clipping of the powers of the Lords, was more inclined to endorse almost any stand taken by Ulster Unionists to thwart the Liberal government.

Ulster Unionists did exploit this potential support by adopting a vigorous campaign in Britain, usually in conjunction with the Southern Irish Unionists. They helped Conservative candidates in by-elections and concentrated money and men in certain marginal seats. Yet in the last analysis they were prepared to stand alone and resist Home Rule, and much thought was given to the mobilisation of Unionist forces in Ulster. With the financial backing of the business community, the Ulster Unionist Council (UUC), since 1905 the organisational hub of Ulster Unionism, laid down plans for opposition to the Third Home Rule Bill. It was agreed that a provisional government of Ulster should be set up in the event of the bill becoming law, and on 25 September 1911 a commission of five was appointed to draw up a constitution. Meantime, great efforts were to be made to sustain Unionist energies in Ulster and to convince the British electorate that Home Rule was unjust and that Ulster Unionists were serious in their determination to remain within the United Kingdom.

It was during this campaign that Craig ceased to be merely a reliable backbencher and emerged in his early forties as a leader, not an inspiring charismatic figure but a masterly director of operations. He had in larger degree than most Ulster Unionists a marked administrative ability, ample reserves of determination, energy and patience and, surprisingly, an eye for the dramatic. Such talents he put at the disposal of Ulster Unionism and more than any one man was responsible for the fact that by the summer of 1914 Ulster Unionists were in a position to resist the imposition of Home Rule in the province.

He was one of the members of the commission appointed to prepare a constitution for the proposed provisional government, but his first real contribution was to ensure that Ulster Unionists had in Edward Carson a leader who was effective in both Ulster and Britain. A vain, hatchet-faced, hypochondriacal but

talented lawyer with a penchant for histrionics, Car-
son was a fervent Unionist from Dublin who had good standing in Britain as a successful barrister and a member of the last Conservative administration. He had become leader of the Irish Unionist Party at Westminster in February 1910, but he needed some persuasion to spearhead Ulster Unionist resistance to the Third Home Rule Bill. 'What I am very anxious about', he wrote to Craig on 29 July 1911, 'is to satisfy myself that the people over there really mean to resist.'[7]

Thereupon Craig set himself to convince Carson of the sincerity of Ulster Unionists. He did this partly, he told his wife, by 'a series of dinners and luncheons' with leaders, but mainly by organising a massive demonstration in the grounds of his own home, Craigavon, on 25 September 1911. There Carson found himself addressing 50,000 men representing all parts of Ulster. They popularly acclaimed him as their leader, and he responded, saying:

> I know the responsibility you are putting on me to-day. In your presence, I cheerfully accept it, grave as it is. And now I enter into a compact with you and everyone of you, and, with the help of God, you and I joined together — I giving you the best I can, and you giving me all your strength behind me — we will yet defeat the most nefarious conspiracy that has ever been hatched against a free people.[8]

Carson got straight to the hearts of Ulster Unionists. His choice as leader was, as one Ulster nobleman put it, 'a capital idea',[9] for which Craig could take full credit. Carson's mercurial temperament and powers of oratory complemented Craig's stability and geniality. As Craig's official biographer has commented, 'Each had what the other lacked. Pooling their resources, they became a third and undeniable per-

son. Effective apart, they were irresistible together.[10]
Carson had the charisma, and Craig had the organising
capacity which Carson so conspicuously lacked. At
times Carson's vanity and constant need for reas-
surance could be trying, but Craig was tolerant and
did not mind that, as Carson himself admitted, 'It was
James Craig who did most of the work, and I got
most of the credit.'[11]

Craig displayed prodigious energy in these years in
presenting and promoting the Ulster Unionist cause in
Ulster and in Britain. The vitality and energy which
enabled him to travel and plot without undue fatigue
leap out from the letters he sent his wife. 'Caught the
4.10 to Kirkintilloch,' he wrote in November 1911,
'had dinner with the chairman, and the meeting
afterwards. It was very noisy, any number of RC's
who interrupted all the time. . . . I got through all
right, but this sort of thing rather takes it out of one.'
In a few weeks in November—December 1911 he
addressed audiences in England, Scotland and Ireland,
crossing the Irish Sea twice. On 7 December he wrote
to his wife from London: 'After the most awful crossing [from Kingstown to Holyhead], a whole gale
blowing, we got there, and I went to Carson and
chatted by his bedside for an hour. He approves of
everything done to date. Met the Committee at 5, and
am dining with J. B. Lonsdale [the secretary of the
Irish Unionist Party at Westminster].' On the following day he wrote: 'To Boss [gunsmith] where I fixed
up an important matter!'[12]

This pace and enthusiasm he maintained over the
years. On 31 July 1912 he reported to his wife:

Yesterday was a very dull day in the House, but I
was busy personally with a multitude of correspondence, committee meetings, interviews with
National school teachers and one body or another

till 8.30. I am now just off to see Salisbury about
speaking in the Ulster Hall on the 27th September
and have eight here for lunch, including Carson. . . .
Then we have Irish estimates all day, and probably
a discussion about the Belfast situation to wind up
with. Among other things, I think I can secure the
Royal Standard carried in front of King William
when he crossed the Boyne.[13]

Craig's contribution to the Ulster Unionist movement was not merely his energy but the fact that he
was able to channel his energy constructively and
purposefully. He realised that efficiency and discipline were essential in the fight against Home Rule.
Unruly mobs could be intimidated and overawed, but
it was harder to coerce a disciplined and organised
community. He also realised how lightly Englishmen
and Irish nationalists regarded threats to resist Home
Rule. 'Nonsense, my dear fellow, nonsense! Rubbish!'
the Chief Secretary said in the Commons in June
1912, and Craig angrily accepted the challenge:

We shall henceforth take the steps which may become necessary to prove to the Government the
sincerity of our people at home — that is, not to
submit to government by the Nationalist Party,
under any circumstances whatever. . . . No one can
say what will happen at this crisis, except that
there is a very strong and earnest determination on
the part of Ulster to take action, and there is a
movement already on foot to take it. If the right
honourable gentleman has challenged this part of
His Majesty's dominions to civil war, then the challenge is accepted![14]

Thus Craig understood the need for dramatic
demonstrations of opinion and accordingly planned
the most famous of Ulster Unionist demonstrations —

the signing of the Solemn League and Covenant. It was a superbly stage-managed affair which underlined the detailed care with which Craig arranged such events and which furthered the Ulster Unionist cause at home and abroad. A pledge by Ulster Unionists to use 'all means which may be found necessary to defeat the present conspiracy to set up a Home Rule Parliament in Ireland',[15] the Covenant acted both as a safety-valve for popular emotion and as evidence to the outside world of the solidarity, determination and self-discipline of Ulster Unionists.

The signing of the Covenant was preceded by a series of meetings beginning in the west, in Enniskillen, the western gateway to Ulster and a frontier town of the plantation, to explain its purpose. At Enniskillen Carson was met by two squadrons of mounted volunteers raised from among the gentry and farmers of Co. Fermanagh, who escorted him to Portora Hill, where 40,000 men of the Unionist Clubs marched past him in military order. The campaign ended with a great eve-of-Covenant rally in the Ulster Hall, Belfast, where Carson was given a faded yellow silk banner which, it was claimed, had been carried before William III at the Battle of the Boyne. It had been obtained by Craig, and this masterstroke created an atmosphere of deep emotion as Carson unfurled the flag and, holding it aloft, exclaimed: 'May this flag ever float over a people that can boast of civil and religious liberty.'[16] Then Craig presented his friend with a silver key, symbolising Ulster as the key to the situation, and a silver pen to sign the Covenant.

Covenant Day, or Ulster Day, 28 September 1912, was declared a public holiday by the UUC, when 237,368 men signed the Covenant and 234,046 women signed a parallel declaration. It was an impressive demonstration of discipline and determination. J. L. Garvin, the editor of *The Observer,* observing

the scenes in Belfast from the top of the City Hall,
[28] wrote:

> Through the mass, with drums and fifes, sashes and
> banners, the clubs marched all day. The streets
> surged with cheering, but still no disorder, still no
> policemen, still no shouts of rage or insult. Yet no-
> one for a moment could have mistaken the concen-
> trated will and courage of these people. They do
> not know what fear and flinching mean in this
> business, and they are not going to know. They do
> not, indeed, believe it possible that they can be
> beaten, but no extremity, the worst, will ever see
> them ashamed.

It was this simple determination that was so awesome.
As Martin Ross, of *Irish RM* fame, wrote of the cere-
mony in one country village, 'Here there was no
hypnotic force of dense masses, no whirlwind of
emotion, only the unadorned and individual action of
those who had left their fields, and taken their lives
and liberties in their hands laying them forth in the
open sunshine as the measure of their resolve.'[17]

By this time Craig had come to realise that something more than peaceful demonstrations was required to underline the resolve of Ulster Unionists
and maintain the momentum of their movement.
Nationalists and Liberals scoffed at their outpourings
as 'Orangeade', and the longer the crisis was prolonged the greater was the danger that the rank and
file would take matters into their own hands. The
answer was the formation of a private army. In January
1912 some Ulster Unionists had begun openly to raise
and drill a military force, keeping within the law by
applying for and obtaining the sanction of two local
magistrates, who were empowered to authorise the
formation of such forces for the purpose of maintaining the constitution of the United Kingdom as then

established. Towards the end of the year the standing committee of the UUC decided that these volunteers should be united into a single body to be known as the Ulster Volunteer Force (UVF). A distinguished retired Indian army officer, Lieutenant-General Sir George Richardson, was appointed commander of the force, which eventually enrolled 90,000 men subject to almost military discipline. Not only was Craig closely involved in the decision to establish the force, but he also guided its development in accordance with the general aims of the movement in his capacity as the UVF's political staff officer.

He was also quick to appreciate that, despite their drilling and military formations, the UVF's image as stern fighters was somewhat marred by their lack of arms. Although Ulster Unionists had been smuggling rifles and ammution for years, the quantities imported had been small and most Volunteers had to parade with wooden rifles enterprisingly supplied in pitch-pine or spruce by a Belfast firm. This lack not only enabled critics to ridicule the Volunteers, but also created discontent among the Volunteers locally and at headquarters. To remedy this situation, Major Fred Crawford, a Belfast businessman, sexist, Unionist fanatic and experienced gun-runner, submitted plans for the large-scale importation of arms. Members of the UUC committee dealing with the question of arms importation had their reservations not only about using the flamboyant Crawford but also about the wisdom of fully arming the UVF, which might precipitate violence and confrontation with Crown forces. However, Craig persuaded them that Crawford was right to stress the psychological effect of equipping the force with modern weapons. In January 1914 Crawford was accordingly authorised to buy arms from Germany and thus embarked upon a thrilling enterprise shrouded in secrecy and bedevilled by

dangers. When, too, the committee began to get cold
[30] feet and instructed Crawford, then on the high seas,
not to land the guns he had obtained but to cruise in
the Baltic for three months, it was Craig who enabled
agreement to be reached between an angry gun-runner
and the cautious committee. Arriving at Craig's home,
where the committee was in session, Crawford looked
like an angry ghost. Dishevelled and ashen and with a
baleful light in his blue eyes, he swept aside Craig's
outstretched hand and declared: 'I will shake hands
with no member of the Committee until I know what
they propose to do with the *Fanny*'s cargo.' Instead
of being offended, Craig put his arms on Crawford's
shoulder and said: 'It's all right, Fred, the Chief is
here.'[18] Thus it was that on the night of 24–25 April
1914 35,000 rifles and 5 million rounds of ammuni-
tion were landed in Ulster and speedily distributed
throughout the province.

Craig's main concern was with, as he told the
Commons on one occasion, his 'trusty friends in the
North of Ireland',[19] but he was not oblivious to the
need to cultivate the Conservative and Unionist Party
in Britain. The Ulster demonstrations were thus also
used to provide a platform for leading British Conservatives and Unionists, the most prominent of whom
was Bonar Law, who on Easter Tuesday 1912 told
100,000 Ulstermen that they were not alone and
that their cause was also the cause of the Empire.
Craig was also concerned to present the Ulster Unionist
case in Britain. Amittedly, Carson bore the brunt of
the parliamentary work, but it was Craig who did
most of the work outside the House, addressing Conservative and Unionist meetings large and small. Walter Long, a former leader of the Irish Unionist Party
and a defeated contender for the leadership of the
Conservative and Unionist Party in 1911, was grateful
to 'My dear Jim' for agreeing to assist in a Wiltshire

constituency, where 'the seat is none too safe, and a speech from you will help us immensely'.[20] The biggest occasion in Britain was a demonstration in July 1912 at Blenheim Palace, the Duke of Marlborough's seat, attended by, among others, some 120 MPs and 40 peers. Craig wrote to his wife that 'They are all making a great fuss about the 19,000 or 20,000 to be here to-day!' Yet, although these numbers were far fewer than those mobilised for demonstrations in Ulster, Craig realised the value of such occasions to Ulster Unionists. On the day after the meeting he told his wife that it had been

> the greatest possible success. The speeches were most comforting to me; I never hoped for such a strong lead from Bonar Law. Carson was grand, and F. E. [Smith] came out splendidly about the Nationalists. The meeting rose to their feet over and over again when good hard hits were made. You will have read everything and easily understood what a relief it is to have our leaders' blessing on what we do, no matter how far we go. . . . It really does put heart into one after such a very encouraging day for Ulster.[21]

This letter typified Craig's preoccupation to make the Ulster Unionist position impregnable. He ran the risk of arrest, but it did not matter to him that plans to defy an act of parliament were scarcely constitutional and totally unbecoming in men who in other circumstances regarded themselves as upholders of the rule of law and who at the time professed their loyalty to the Crown, constitution and Empire. Craig, along with other Ulster Unionists, though that almost any means of resistance was justified. It was argued that the Home Rule policy violated the convention that parliamentary democracy must depend upon due respect for the convictions of minorities, and that the

constitution was in suspense, since the Parliament Act
[32] prevented the House of Lords from submitting the question to the electorate. As Craig told the Commons, 'The Government is not to be treated as a Government, but as a caucus, led by rebels.'[22]

Craig's defiance, self-righteous and devoid of doubt, was fully in keeping with the Presbyterian tradition which had helped to shape his character and political thought. That tradition was characterised by political radicalism, anti-establishment feeling, experience of persecution, intransigence and even rebellion. Indeed, political thinking among Ulster Protestants had scarcely developed since the covenanting days of the seventeenth century, when contractual theories of government had been in vogue. The result was that Ulster Protestants and Unionists maintained that citizens owed only conditional allegiance to the government and that rebellion was perfectly justifiable should the government be deemed to be failing in its duty towards its citizens, or any group of them. This tradition was the essential and unique feature of Craig's political make-up which distinguished him from most political leaders in Britain and all in the South of Ireland. It explains both his serious intention of undertaking a rebellion against the Third Home Rule Bill and the fact that British politicians and Irish nationalist leaders thought he was bluffing, for they could not appreciate that the spirit of the Covenanters could survive in a respectable Tory leader. This is why Craig's contribution to Ulster's resistance was greater and more positive than Carson's. Not only was he the more capable organiser, but he also had a more certain sense of purpose. He had none of the doubts which constantly tormented the Anglican Carson as to the moral and constitutional rectitude of the course they were pursuing.

Craig's vital contribution to Ulster Unionism at this

time was acknowledged both in private and in public. After Ulster Day, Viscount Castlereagh, later 7th Marquess of Londonderry and Northern Ireland's first Minister of Education, wrote to Mrs Craig that 'James is to be congratulated on a splendid piece of organisation.'[23] Two years later a postcard was published showing the uniformed Craig with a sword in his right hand, his left foot on a prostrate and wriggling John Redmond, the leader of the Nationalist Party, and his left hand holding aloft an aghast Asquith, the Prime Minister. The verse beneath the picture read:

> He who volunteered for England in her deadly
> Boer war
> Is for Ulster volunteering a treason plot to mar;
> By his voice in Britain's Parliament he has fought
> the deadly foe,
> By his sword in loyal Ulster he'll lay treason
> mongers low,
> Then hurragh for Craig and Ulster, with a hip, hip,
> hip hurray!
> With men like him and Carson we're quite ready
> for the fray.[24]

The Ulster Unionist campaign not only marked Craig out as a leading Unionist in Britain as well as Ulster, it also marked Ulster out for special treatment. By the summer of 1914, when the Third Home Rule Bill had completed its parliamentary circuits, Ulster Unionists were in a position to form their own provisional government, protected by an armed and disciplined volunteer force, which, in turn, was backed by an indemnity fund in aid of those likely to be disabled, widowed and orphaned should any attempt be made to force Home Rule on the province.

The latter contingency was unlikely. While the campaign did not succeed in killing the policy of Home Rule once and for all, it did focus attention on

the Ulster question and generated in Britain a good
deal of sympathy for the Ulster Unionist case against
Home Rule. There developed in Britain a feeling that
while it would be unfair to allow Ulster Unionists to
deprive the rest of Ireland of Home Rule, it would be
equally unfair, if not impossible, to force Home Rule
and a Dublin parliament on Ulster. From the late summer of 1913 onwards serious consideration was given
to the problem of reconciling the fears of Ulster
Unionists with the aspirations of Irish nationalists.
At first there was a good deal of shadow-boxing, but
by the early summer of 1914 the idea of partition,
the exclusion of Ulster from the jurisdiction of a
Dublin parliament, was firmly established.

Partition was less acceptable to Carson than to
Craig and other Ulster Unionists. Carson, a Southerner,
felt some responsibility towards the scattered loyalist
minority in the South and had hoped to use the Ulster
question, the weakest point in the case for Home
Rule, to kill Home Rule and so maintain the Union in
its entirety. Craig and most Ulster Unionists, on the
other hand, had no such compunction about throw-
ing over the Southern Unionists, whom they had long
regarded as cowardly if not stupid. Thus although it
had been intended that the Ulster provisional government should act with due regard for loyalists in the
rest of Ireland, the common bonds of Unionism and
Protestantism were insufficient to overcome the
attractions of partition. Craig and his followers quickly
perceived the logic and advantages of dividing Ireland.
If they could not save the whole country for the
Empire, they could at least save themselves.

Yet, although the idea of partition had been established, no agreement could be reached on such crucial
details as the area of Ulster to be excluded from Dublin rule and whether such exclusion should be tem-
porary or permanent. Questions such as these caused

the breakdown of the Buckingham Palace Conference, an all-party gathering summoned in July 1914 by King George V in the hope of reaching a settlement. Craig along with Carson represented the Ulster Unionists, but they felt unable to accept less than the permanent exclusion of the entire province of Ulster. Just as Redmond, under pressure from his followers, wanted the smallest possible area exluded from Dublin rule for the shortest possible time, so Carson and Craig were under pressure from their followers to accept only a clean-cut exclusion of the whole province, and during the conference they received a series of telegrams exhorting them to honour the Covenant. 'Fellow Covenanters in Monaghan', they were told, 'expect you to stand firm, better fight than break Covenant.'[25]

The deadlock and drift to civil war were broken only by the outbreak of the First World War on 4 August 1914. Under cover of a party truce, the Home Rule Bill was put on the statute book on 18 September, but its operation was suspended until the end of the war and the Ulster Unionist position safeguarded. Asquith dismissed as absolutely unthinkable any notion of the coercion of Ulster and promised that before the Home Rule Act came into operation an amending bill would be introduced. Craig did not like this procedure, but at least it ensured that when the Irish question was taken out of cold storage Ulster would receive special consideration.

3

The outbreak of the First World War in August 1914 not only brought to an end the crisis over the Third Home Rule Bill, it also provided Craig and the Ulster Unionists with an opportunity to demonstrate their loyalty to the Empire. It was Craig's idea that the

services of the UVF should be offered as a fighting
unit on any front, and it was he who persuaded Lord
Kitchener, the War Secretary, that the UVF should
form the nucleus of a special Ulster Division, the 36th,
of the British army. Craig, still on the reserve of
officers, became a lieutenant-colonel and the new
division's Assistant Adjutant and Quartermaster-
General. Characteristically, immediately after his
crucial interview with Kitchener at the War Office,
he sped to Moss Brothers to buy uniforms for his new
troops. Much to his disappointment, Craig's efforts
on behalf of the Ulster Division had to be confined
to recruitment and equipment, for poor health prevented him from accompanying the division abroad,
where it was all but annihilated at Thiepval in July
1916. Repeated efforts to pass a medical board failed,
and in April 1916 Craig reluctantly resigned his commission.

Unable to serve with the fighting forces abroad,
Craig resumed his career in British politics. When
Lloyd George formed the second wartime coalition in
December 1916, Carson joined the cabinet as First
Lord of the Admiralty, and Craig received minor office
as Treasurer of the Household and a whip. Further
recognition followed in the 1917 new year's honours
list, when he received a baronetcy, but his steady progress was interrupted by a dispute between Ulster
Unionists and other members of the Irish Convention,
summoned by Lloyd George in June 1917 to solve
the Irish question. Carson's presence in the cabinet
was embarrassing the government's attempts to grapple
with the problems created by the refusal of the Ulster
Unionist delegation to accept an all-Ireland parliament, and after consulting Craig, Carson decided to
resign. Craig had no alternative but to resign also. 'I
have been so intimately associated with him [Carson]
in Irish affairs', he wrote to Lloyd George in his letter

of resignation, 'that it is quite impossible for me to separate myself from him in the action he has now taken; and as my reliance on his judgement is so unqualified . . . I feel I have no choice but to ask you to accept my resignation.'[26] His resignation enabled him to speak freely on Irish affairs in the Commons, particularly on the need for conscription, but it did not ruin his chances of future office. In January 1919 he was appointed Parliamentary Secretary of the Ministry of Pensions in Lloyd George's new peacetime coalition. Craig, who never failed to respond to the needs of serving soldiers, quickly familiarised himself with the complicated technicalities of a ministry which had been allowed to drift into chaos. The appointment was a popular one. When he rose to reply to his first parliamentary question, he was received with loud and friendly cheers and impressed observers with his dignified and courteous manner. As a matter of fact, commented one large provincial newspaper, 'Those who really know Sir James have long recognised in him an extremely clever man, whose parliamentary qualities have long been over-shadowed by the fact that he has very largely confined his activities to Irish affairs.'[27] Early promotion was forecast.

Perhaps because he lacked the flair which would have compensated for his inexperience, the promotion Craig eventually received was less elevated than some commentators had expected. On 2 April 1920 he was appointed to another junior post, this time as Financial Secretary to the Admiralty, under his friend and former leader of the Irish Unionist Party, Walter Long, the First Lord. Since, however, Long was gravely ill for much of the latter part of 1920, Craig was in effect First Lord, and his handling of business underlined his administrative ability, his bluff common sense and his utter kindliness. An important innovation in the preparation of naval estimates simplied the

work of the House by presenting as a matter of course
a mass of information which in the past had had to be
extorted by question and answer across the floor. He
kept within bounds a developing rumpus over the
revelation that the officer commanding one of His
Majesty's warships had entertained on board ship a
Bolshevik general. It was a matter for the First Lord,
but a wrathful Lloyd George, horrified by adverse
publicity, intervened and seemed bent on mobilising
the whole navy to discuss the matter with him at
Downing Street. It was probably fortunate that the
irascible Long was ill, for he would have brooked no
interference and would at least have threatened
resignation, but Craig calmed the storm with 'the
patience of Job and the imperturbability of the equa-
tor'. 'My endeavour', he wrote to the anxious Long,
'is to persuade the Prime Minister that it is most
important to leave the exercise of such discretion in
the hands of individual Officers Commanding, and
that if the discretion has been unwisely used in this
particular instance, you will take the necessary steps
to deal with the Officer in question.' Finally, Craig
managed to run the Admiralty without offending its
absent chief. Long very much appreciated the courtesy
and scrupulous care with which he was kept informed
of events. 'I am extremely grateful to you', he wrote
to Craig on 10 November 1920, 'for . . . the really
wonderful way in which you steer us through difficulties and avoid trouble of any kind'; and on the
following day he thanked Craig for 'the tact, firmness
and courage with which you have dealt with every
difficulty'.[28] These were just the sort of problems
Craig was most suited to resolve. Immediate, limited
and personal, they required little political insight or
long-term planning.

Ironically, it was at this point that Craig's further
progress in British politics was halted by the success

of the movement to which he had contributed so much. By the Government of Ireland Act, 1920, [39] Ulster Unionists received their reward for years of determined opposition to Home Rule. That act, introduced at Westminster in February 1920 and finally passed in the following December, provided for the partition of Ireland into the six counties of Northern Ireland and the twenty-six counties of Southern Ireland, and the establishment in each area of similar parliaments with limited powers of Home Rule.

As a member, albeit a junior one, of the coalition government which proposed the new measure, Craig did have an opportunity to influence the bill in the interests of Ulster Unionism. He was sometimes involved in cabinet discussions of Irish affairs, when he was always looked to for the presentation of the Ulster Unionist point of view, and his opportunity for influence increased when he moved to the Admiralty, since his chief there, Long, was also chairman of the cabinet's Irish Situation Committee. However, Craig never acted in isolation from his fellow-Unionists in the North, but was always ready to consult with other leaders there, particularly Richard (later Sir Richard) Dawson Bates, the secretary of the UUC, upon whose views he placed much reliance. When first informed in November 1919 of the government's intention to introduce a new bill, Craig asked permission to consult Bates, who, he told one cabinet minister, 'knew the mind of Ulster better than almost anyone else'.[29]

There were some matters on which neither Craig nor Ulster Unionists at large had any influence, most notably the decision to set up a parliament in the North as well as one in the South. Ulster Unionists had never asked for a parliament of their own and had assumed that in the event of their exclusion from the authority of a Dublin parliament they would continue to be ruled directly from Westminster. Such direct rule over the North was, however, unacceptable [40] to the imperial government. It hoped to withdraw from Ireland as completely as possible, while at the same time redeeming pledges to Ulster Unionists and satisfying, as far as was consistent with imperial interests, the claims of Irish nationalists. The establishment of a parliament in Northern Ireland was therefore preferable to simple exclusion, since it would be less objectionable to nationalist opinion. Moreover, the government somewhat perversely hoped that the establishment of two equal Irish parliaments would foster Irish unity.

Although they had never asked for a parliament of their own, Craig along with other Ulster Unionists nevertheless saw the advantage of having a regional parliament. With a parliament of their own they felt they would be more secure than if they remained directly under Westminster. British politicians and opinion, absorbed in the problems of post-war reconstruction, had little time for Irish affairs, and there was no longer any serious opposition in Great Britain to Home Rule. In a Westminster parliament Ulster Unionists would be subject to constant attacks by sections of the Liberal Party and the developing Labour Party, which might one day form a government. Moreover, Unionists in Britain now acknowledged Ulster Unionist claims for special consideration in a spirit of resignation rather than enthusiasm, with a stoical determination to honour a debt rather than a burning desire to reward their Ulster friends. Ulster Unionists therefore feared that any attempt by a Labour or Liberal government to force them to join with the South would meet very little resistance in Britain. Craig's brother Charles, the MP for South Antrim, summed up James's feelings and those of Ulster Unionists in general when he told the Commons on 29 March 1920:

We would much prefer to remain part and parcel of the United Kingdom. We have prospered, we have made our province prosperous under the Union, and under the laws passed by this House and administered by officers appointed by this House. . . . We do not in any way desire to recede from a position which has been in every way satisfactory to us, but we have many enemies in this country, and we feel that an Ulster without a Parliament of its own would not be in nearly as strong a position as one in which a Parliament had been set up where the Executive had been appointed and where above all the paraphernalia of Government was already in existence. We believe that so long as we were without a Parliament of our own constant attacks would be made upon us, and constant attempts would be made . . . to draw us into a Dublin Parliament. . . . We profoundly distrust the Labour party and we profoundly distrust the right hon. gentleman for Paisley (Mr Asquith). We believe that if either of those parties, or the two in combination, were once more in power our chances of remaining a part of the United Kingdom would be very small indeed. We see our safety, therefore, in having a Parliament of our own, for we believe that once a Parliament is set up and working well . . . we should fear no one, and we feel we would then be in a position of absolute security . . . and therefore I say that we prefer to have a Parliament, although we do not want one of our own.[30]

In other respects, however, Craig helped to shape the Government of Ireland Bill in accordance with Ulster Unionists' interests and wishes. Originally the bill had provided only for single-chamber legislatures in the North and South, but, under pressure from Southern Unionists, the House of Lords amended it

so as to provide for the establishment of second
[42] chambers in order to accommodate dissentient minorities. Ulster Unionists did not see the need for a second
chamber of the Northern parliament, because they
thought the Catholic/nationalist minority in the North
would have adequate representation in the Commons;
and anyway they regarded second chambers as un-
democratic. Although they could hardly refuse to
accept a second chamber, they did insist that it should
be as harmless as possible, and on 5 November 1920
Craig was able to relay to imperial ministers such as
Long the results the 'many long and anxious con-
ferences'[31] held on the subject by Ulster Unionist MPs.
The result was that whereas the Southern Senate was
designed to provide reasonable representation for the
Southern minority, the Northern Senate merely reflected the Unionist majority in the Commons. The
differences between the two Senates provoked Joe
Devlin, the Northern Nationalist leader, to complain
that 'Of all the dishonest transactions that I have
ever heard of in my life, this Senate arrangement is
the most dishonest.'[32]

More vitally, Craig played a crucial role in deter-
mining that Northern Ireland should consist of only
six of the nine counties of the historic province of
Ulster. Ever since partition had first been mooted the
most serious bone of contention had been what part
of Ulster should be exempt from Dublin rule. It was
an almost intractable problem because the Protestant
and Unionist population was concentrated in certain
counties. Only four counties had Protestant majorities,
and within each county religious and political affilia-
tions were unevenly distributed. Such figures might
have justified a four-counties split, but partition was
usually discussed in terms of the six counties of
Antrim, Armagh, Down, Fermanagh, Londonderry
and Tyrone, in which Protestants formed 66 per cent

of the population, or the entire nine counties of Ulster, where Protestants comprised only 57 per cent of the population. According to the 1911 census, the nine counties contained 890,880 non-Catholics and 690,816 Catholics, but the Unionist majority was larger in the six counties, where there were 820,370 non-Catholics and 430,161 Catholics.

The imperial government was in two minds on the matter. The six counties would be the more stable unit, but there were attractions in a nine-counties split. The whole province of Ulster was a more logical geographical unit; a nine-counties split would be easier to defend in parliament; and, with its large Catholic/nationalist minority, a nine-counties Northern Ireland would the more readily facilitate the ultimate reunification of Ireland. After much deliberation and consulation the cabinet's Irish Situation Committee, charged with drawing up the bill, came down on 17 February 1920 in favour of 'Ulster as against the six counties', but a week later the cabinet reversed the decision. The reason for the change was that a nine-counties split was unacceptable to the Ulster Unionist leadership. It would therefore, the cabinet concluded, 'be difficult for the Government to force through a scheme which was unacceptable both to their friends and to their critics'.[33]

Craig was in a large degree responsible for this decision. He and a number of other leading Ulster Unionists were convinced that only a six-counties split would provide adequate security for Unionists. A six-counties parliament with fifty-two seats would contain a safe Unionist majority of between ten and twenty. The situation in a nine-counties parliament, on the other hand, would be precarious, for counties Cavan, Donegal and Monaghan contained only some 70,000 Protestants but 260,000 Catholics. Estimates varied. Proponents of a six-counties split thought that at best a nine-counties parliament would yield a Unionist majority of three or four, although one estimate suggested that, owing to the growth of the socialist vote in and around Belfast, Unionists could possibly be in a minority of two. In any case, the Unionist majority in a nine-counties parliament would be so slender that 'no sane man would undertake to carry on a Parliament with it. . . . A couple of Members sick, or two or three Members absent for some accidental reason, might in one evening hand over the entire Ulster Parliament and the entire Ulster position' to the South. 'A dreadful thing to contemplate,' said Craig's brother Charles.[34]

Craig ensured that this determination not to have a nine-counties parliament was known to the imperial cabinet. Thus, before the cabinet meeting which finally decided in favour of the six counties, Craig had a long conversation with Lloyd George, in which he emphasised to the Prime Minister the necessity for a six-counties split. The cabinet wisely agreed that 'A scheme which was advocated both by Sir James Craig, a representative Ulsterman, and Sir J. O'Connor, who could speak for the Irish hierarchy, would be likely to meet with a better reception than one which they both condemned.'*[35]

Craig had not only to press the case for a six-counties split on the imperial government, but he also had to help persuade the majority of Ulster Unionists to accept it and throw over the other three counties of the province. Although a six-counties split

*Another suggestion made by Craig during his discussions with imperial ministers was the establishment of a Boundary Commission to determine the border between the North and the South, by which no doubt he hoped to secure a larger but more homogeneous area. The cabinet was attracted by the idea but did not pursue it in case it led to unrest. This was probably the origin of the Boundary Commission which, much to the horror of Craig and his supporters, was provided for two years later under the Anglo-Irish Treaty.

had the full backing of the Unionist leadership and businessmen in and around Belfast, it met with a good deal of opposition not only from Unionists in Counties Cavan, Donegal and Monaghan, which would all go to the South, but also from Ulster Unionists at large. They rejected all the arguments against a nine-counties parliament, especially the view that the parties would be too finely balanced. Nine-counties men thought it absurd to imagine that a province with a Protestant majority of 200,064 should not be able to return a majority of MPs. They did not merely condemn a six-counties split as a betrayal of Unionists in the excluded three counties and a violation of the Covenant, which had applied to all of Ulster. They also produced some wide-ranging and thoughtful arguments in support of their case, which emphasised the geographical and economic unity of the province and insisted that a six-counties parliament would be too parochial and contain an unheathily large Unionist majority. 'The ideal position', they maintained, 'would be to have a fairly strong Nationalist minority in the North and a fairly strong Unionist minority in the South. If this ideal position cannot at present be effected in the South it can and should be in the North.'[36]

Some of these arguments had been rehearsed in 1916, when, following the Easter Rising, Lloyd George had attempted an Irish settlement on the basis of partition and the implementation of the suspended 1914 Home Rule Act. Then the UUC, at the urging of Carson and Craig, had accepted the principle of a six-counties split in order to assist a settlement and thus forward the war effort, and the problem of deserting the other three counties had been overcome by allowing the decision to depend upon their Unionist inhabitants, who manfully accepted the partition of Ulster as 'a patriotic act of self-sacrifice'.[37] In 1920, however, no such concessions were made to sentiment. [46] Craig and the Ulster Unionist leadership were determined to have the six counties. When in March 1920 the UUC decided to accept but take no responsibility for the 1920 bill, an amendment in favour of a nine-counties Northern Ireland created an extraordinarily difficult and tense position, in which a false step or a wrong note would have brought chaos. Yet Craig was master of the situation. Speaking with the authority of a member of the imperial government, privy to its thinking on Irish affairs, he emphasised that the establishment by statute of a six-counties Northern Ireland offered the only permanent bulwark against Irish unity and the removal of the whole of Ireland from the Empire. Craig thus not only secured the defeat of the nine-counties amendment, but also, according to Herbert Dixon, the future Chief Whip, 'left a permanent feeling of confidence in the honest intentions of the Government'. Dixon was right to congratulate Craig on 'the magnificent way you handled the situation. . . . From a personal point of view, you scored nothing less than a triumph.' The position remained tense and dangerous, but, Dixon added, 'If the Government meet the people fairly, and hold on the course you have mapped out, I believe things will right themselves.'[38]

A residue of bitterness did remain. There was a feeling that matters had been rushed through by a Belfast clique and that the three counties had been 'thrown to the wolves with very little compunction'. Unionists in these counties felt 'betrayed and deserted', while some Unionists in other parts of Ulster felt 'shamed and dishonoured'.[39] It was fortunate for Craig's future in Northern Ireland that such resentments were directed not against him but against Carson, the nominal leader of the Ulster Unionists.

Not only did Craig help to shape some of the crucial

details of the 1920 Government of Ireland Bill, but he also threw whatever influence he had behind those imperial ministers who wanted to persevere with it despite opposition to it in the South. As the dominant party there since 1918, Sinn Féin, flatly refused to acknowledge the existence of the 'Partition Bill', as it was contemptuously called, the imperial government's Irish experts were sometimes inclined to advise the abandonment of the bill and its replacement by an offer of 'Dominion Home Rule'. Craig's view, however, when he attended a cabinet discussion of Irish policy on 23 July 1920, was that 'the Bill ought to be pushed quickly through Parliament'.[40]

Craig was also able to use his position as a junior minister to rebut the many charges levelled against Ulster Unionists by critics of the 1920 bill. A particular cause for concern during the passage of the bill was the spread of the Anglo-Irish War to the North and the consequent growth of subversion and unrest there. In some rural areas the UVF began to regroup for self-protection, while the state of Belfast, with its rioting, expulsion of Catholics from their work and other sectarian happenings, was reported by the Liberal and Labour press in Britain in such a way as to make nonsense of the Ulster Unionist claim to represent the most progressive and civilised elements in Irish life. According to the *Daily Herald* on 31 August 1920,

> The bloody harvest of Carsonism is being reaped in Belfast. . . . The gangs who have organised the reign of terror are the very people who protest they are afraid that *they* would, under even partial Home Rule, be persecuted and denied religious liberty.

Craig was quick to put the Ulster Unionist reply to such charges in two memoranda he submitted to the cabinet at the beginning of September 1920. Sinn

Féin, he claimed, was working in conjunction with
Bolsheviks to establish a republic hostile to the
British Empire, and, owing to its growth, almost
unopposed by the Crown forces, the 'Loyalist rank
and file have determined to take action so that their
safety depends on themselves'. 'So desperate' did the
Ulster Unionist leadership regard the situation that

> Unless the Government will take immediate action,
> it may be advisable for them to see what steps can
> be taken towards a system of *organised* reprisals
> against the rebels, mainly in order to defeat them,
> but partly to restrain their own followers from
> acts which are regrettable, and in large measure
> ineffective.

The answer, Craig suggested, was the utilisation of a
revived and reorganised UVF, for 'Where the Ulster
Volunteer units have retained their arms, no serious
disturbances have hitherto arisen.'[41] It was this suggestion that eventually led in the following November to
the formation of the Ulster Special Constabulary,
which became Northern Ireland's main peace-keeping
force in the early years of the new region's existence.

4

Once the Government of Ireland Act had received the
royal assent on 23 December 1920, the question that
excited much talk in the North was who would
become the first Prime Minister of Northern Ireland.
The choice lay between Carson and Craig, the two
men who, in so far as individuals can influence events,
were responsible for the establishment of Northern
Ireland. Carson was the official leader of the Ulster
Unionists, but he had few administrative talents, was
ill and ageing, and, despite his vanity, knew that the
responsibilities of the premiership would be beyond

him. Craig was the obvious candidate and emerged as official leader of the Ulster Unionists and Northern Ireland's first Prime Minister after a graceful little charade had been acted out. On 25 January 1921 a formal invitation to accept the premiership was made to Carson in the knowledge that it would be refused, and on the following day the standing committee of the UUC unanimously invited Craig to submit himself for appointment as Prime Minister of Northern Ireland. Thereupon, to quote his official biographer, 'Craig decided to go home.'[42]

3
Statemaker

All my political career has been bound up with
Ulster, and this Act is the culmination of all my
humble efforts. Was I then to say, Take your act,
I will stay in London, and while you work the Act
I will look on. If it was a success I would thank
God for it, but if it broke down and was a failure,
after all the efforts of my colleagues and myself, I
would go to my grave ashamed if I did not go
down with the ship too.[1]

Thus was the spirit in which Craig accepted in his
fifty-first year the post of Northern Ireland's first
Prime Minister — out of a sense of duty rather than in
anticipation of personal fulfilment.

He had enjoyed junior office in the imperial government and would probably have achieved cabinet rank,
but he sacrificed both his post at the Admiralty and
his seat in the imperial parliament to become Prime
Minister of Northern Ireland. His last day at the
Admiralty and the House at Westminster, 21 March
1921, was a sad one, and in the evening his wife had
'never seen him so depressed, as he is always so
philosophical, and says one should never dwell on
what is done with but concentrate on the present and
the future'.[2] The future, he hoped, would be a bright
one. His government would, he pledged, be 'at the
disposal of the people of Northern Ireland' and
would only have in view 'the welfare of the people'.

Its duty and privilege would be

[51]

> to look to the people as a whole, to set ourselves to
> probe to the bottom those problems that have
> retarded progress in the past, to do everything that
> lies in our power to help forward developments in
> town and country. . . . We will be cautious in our
> legislation. We will be absolutely honest and fair in
> administering the law.[3]

It was not, however, the future which most preoccupied Craig in 1921–22 but the pressing demands
of the present, which threatened the very existence of
Northern Ireland. Craig rose to these immediate challenges, and it was due to him that the new regional
government began to operate in the North and
emerged, albeit not unscathed, from the threatened
anarchy of those early months.

1

The creation of an apparatus of state was the first
task facing Craig, particularly the formation of government departments. Under the Union the powers of
government in Ireland had been distributed among
some thirty different departments, and the problem
was how these powers could be most efficiently
grouped in Northern Ireland without producing too
many office-holders in parliament. The donkey-work
in resolving this problem was undertaken by Sir Ernest
Clark, the Assistant Under-Secretary in Northern Ireland, but he acted in the closest consultation with
Craig, who took an intense interest in the shaping of
ministries. After administrative convenience had been
weighed against political expediency, the scheme of
government announced towards the end of May 1921
contained seven departments: the Prime Minister's,
which was to co-ordinate activities in Northern Ireland and act as a channel of communication with the

imperial government; and the Ministries of Finance,
Home Affairs, Education, Labour, Agriculture and
Commerce.

The choice of ministers to head these departments
gave Craig considerable worry. The plain truth was
that there was a dearth of political talent in a movement which for so long had had only a single and
negative aim and had developed no constructive
philosophy to help it take responsibility for a government it had neither wanted nor expected. Nevertheless, many Unionists were in such a state of official
pregnancy that there was always the temptation to
buy off potential opposition by recruiting extremists,
particularly for junior posts. Although Craig resisted
this temptation, his ultimate choice of cabinet ministers was determined not by any long-term political
programme or vision of the future, but rather reflected
his desire to reward past services to the cause and to
balance the various sectional and geographical interests
of the province. The Minister of Home Affairs, Richard
Dawson Bates, a solicitor, had been since 1905
honorary secretary of the UUC and had thus been
closely involved in the organisation of resistance to
Home Rule. John Miller Andrews, a linen-manu-
facturer and chairman of the Ulster Unionist Labour
Association, became Minister of Labour, while
Hugh McDowell Pollock, a flour-importer and the
Ulster Unionists' leading financial expert, became
Minister of Finance. The east of the province was
represented by the Minister of Education, the 7th
Marquess of Londonderry, who owned much land
in Co. Down and had held junior office at West-
minster; while the west was represented by a man
from an old Co. Fermanagh family, Edward Mervyn
Archdale, who had long served as a Westminster MP
and who initially took charge of the Ministries of
Agriculture and Commerce.

Most of these were good initial appointments, lending dignity, weight and talent to the new government. Pollock, although sixty-nine, was an impressive man with a fine mind. Andrews was conscientious, energetic and humane. Londonderry may often have stood on his dignity and have spent too much time looking after his interests in England, but he was respected and had broader views than the rest of Ulster Unionists. Archdale was not bearing his sixty-eight years at all well, but his long experience at Westminster enabled him to preside decently over a talented and energetic set of officials, at least in Agriculture, who more than compensated for their minster's deficiencies.

Bates's appointment as Minister of Home Affairs was, unfortunately, less happy. His was a key ministry, involving responsibility for some of the most controversial questions in Northern Ireland, such as electoral affairs, local government and law and order, but Bates, a small man physically and intellectually, was unable to give such questions the careful and sympathetic handling they so urgently required. He looked upon all Catholics as nationalists and regarded all nationalists not just as political enemies but as traitors. His previous work as an Ulster Unionist organiser had been, to quote Lord Londonderry, 'no training for the duties of Home Secretary and his support and standing in the Six Counties was not high enough to give him that general support and confidence which are such factors in successfully controlling a Government office'.[4] Moreover, the attitude of his subordinates did little to mitigate Bates's partisanship or broaden his outlook. His first Parliamentary Secretary, Robert Dick Megaw, a barrister, could be the most uncompromising of Unionists, while experience of Dublin Castle methods had given his first Permanent Secretary, Samuel Watt, a less than disinterested attitude on questions affecting law and order. Watt shared [54] the Ulster Unionist view that special crimes legislation should not be used, as he once protested, 'against those who are loyal to the Crown'.[5]

Craig also helped to determine the nature of the parliament of Northern Ireland. Of course, its size and powers had been laid down by the Government of Ireland Act, but Craig did initially strive to ensure that it would be a credit to the six counties. It was at his insistence that its procedures were largely modelled upon those of Westminster. Whether such pomp and formality were appropriate to a small regional assembly is a matter for debate, but one of Craig's biographers justified the decision by arguing that although 'some very queer fish have been elected to Stormont', it had 'never declined to the depths' of the Southern Dáil, where 'the stench of stale ideas' and 'the smell of foul gas escaping from the speeches' offended the nostrils of respectable Southern Irishmen.[6]

In the same pursuit of dignity and standing, Craig tried to ensure that the Unionist members of the first parliament were, as he was relieved to tell the Chief Secretary on 16 April 1921, 'most fit and proper persons all along the line'.[7] The general election, which took place on Empire Day, 24 May 1921, was not only the first in Northern Ireland but also the first general election in the United Kingdom to be held under PR. Thus candidates and the campaign had to be organised with particular care. The brunt of this work was borne by the Chief Whip, Herbert Dixon, a Westminster MP of long standing, but Craig took a great deal of interest in the selection of candidates, urging potentially useful men to stand for election and helping to resolve selection disputes which might have resulted in Independents splitting the Unionist vote. Not only would good official Unionist candidates assist the reputation of Northern Ireland, but they would also help to consolidate Craig's own leadership, for he wrote on 22 April 1921 to the former leader, Carson:

Just as you will recollect, a certain period was necessary before you yourself felt that you had gained the real position of leader and were comfortable in the saddle, so I, hopefully steadily gaining ground, know well that it will take some considerable time for the whole of the people to recognise this change in the life of Ulster.[8]

This consideration, together with the inexperience of most of the Unionist candidates with both parliamentary elections and the problems posed by PR, meant that Craig had to be particularly active in the election campaign. Indeed, he adopted an almost presidential style, telling one meeting of Co. Down Unionists:

If Ulster listens to me, and if Ulster believes in me, as I believe she does, I will carry them through, and I will win this contest and sweep the six counties for loyalty as against the Republic. Go into the fight feeling that you have in yourselves got the salvation and in me you have a leader, who will never desert you and who will never betray you.[9]

The campaign revolved entirely around the question of partition. This had not been Craig's intention, for he had made a dramatic attempt to eliminate the issue. He had hoped that recognition by the South of Northern Ireland's position would bring peace to the six counties, and to that end he was willing to talk directly with nationalist leaders in the South, against the advice of his colleagues and the wishes of his supporters. His first meeting with a Sinn Féin leader, Eamon de Valera, on 5 May 1921, was a theatrically clandestine but dangerous affair. The idea for the

meeting had orginated with 'Andy' Cope, Assistant
Under-Secretary at Dublin Castle, who believed that a
settlement of Irish problems could be achieved by
methods more appropriate to stories in *Boys' Own
Paper.* On the pretext of visiting the Lord Lieutenant,
Craig travelled down to Dublin and was eventually
escorted to a secret destination by 'three of the
worst looking toughs I have ever seen'. The confrontation was tense and achieved nothing. Craig seemed to
de Valera 'anxious and ill at ease', while Craig thought
that the latter had 'very much the look of a hunted
man'. It was hardly a union of hearts and minds.
Craig complained that de Valera spent almost the
whole time 'harping on grievances of Ireland for the
past 700 years instead of coming down to practical
present-day discussion', although the Sinn Féin
leader's biographers claim that this account is 'hardly
fair' and that de Valera talked mainly about the Act
of Union.[10] In any case, even had some agreement
emerged, it is doubtful whether it would have been
acceptable to Ulster Unionists suspicious of anything
emanating from the South, for on his return to Belfast
Craig was 'met by various palefaced, nervy, agitated
people, all thinking he had made a fearful mistake'.[11]

Perhaps his followers were 'nervy' and 'agitated'
because they had got wind of ill-founded rumours
later circulating in Dublin to the effect that Craig
had gone to Dublin to ask de Valera to become
Prime Minister of a united Ireland. Such a notion
was preposterous. It is true that Craig's view of partition was somewhat different from that of his colleagues and supporters, to whom the very thought
of a united Ireland was anathema. Unlike them, he
was willing to contemplate the prospect of the
eventual reunification of the country. He himself
never intended to lead Ulster into a Dublin parliament, nor to sit in one, but he did not rule out the

possibility that one day Ulster might be persuaded — but not forced — to participate in an all-Ireland parlia- ment, in which case he would do nothing to prevent it. There was, however, as far as Craig was concerned, no immediate prospect of unity. His 'exact position' was, as he told Michael Collins in January 1922, that

> For the present an all-Ireland Parliament was out of the question, possibly in years to come — 10, 20, or 50 years — Ulster might be tempted to join with the South. . . . He would do nothing to prevent an all-Ireland Parliament, and . . . if he were convinced it were in the interests of the people of Ulster, he would frankly tell them of his views, but should such an eventuality arise, he would not feel justi-fied himself in taking part in an all-Ireland Parlia-ment. 'He would erect no barriers round a Dublin Parliament, but in no case would he pass through them himself.'[12]

Meantime, talk of unity was nonsense and sugges-tions that Northern Ireland should surrender its status or any of its territory, as defined in the 1920 act, were, Craig argued, irresponsible. Throughout the early months he was determined to maintain Northern Ireland's borders and its status as part of the United Kingdom. His slogan 'Not an inch' sub-stantially reflected his attitude to the border. He was willing to consider minor rectifications, but he roundly rejected any notion that substantial areas of Northern Ireland should be transferred to the South.

As the years went by, Craig became more intran-sigent, both in theory and in practice, on the question of partition, but such intransigence scarcely justifies the charges levelled against him by Irish nationalists and their sympathisers that he was an enemy of Ire-land and a mere tool of the English. Partitionist though he was, Craig bore the South no malice or ill-will. On

the contrary, in his optimistic moments he was in-
clined to think of the two parts of Ireland as sisters, striving against each other in friendly competition, and throughout his premiership he thought that it was in the North's interest to maintain friendly relations with the South, not least because a secure border would facilitate peace in Northern Ireland. More-over, when he did not feel threatened, Craig could be positively benevolent towards the South, especially in the matter of relations with Britain. North and South often had similar difficulties in their dealings with Westminster, and Craig's empathy with Southern leaders engaged in negotiations with imperial ministers was evident in the sound and helpful advice he gave to de Valera in July 1921 and in his remark to Kevin O'Higgins in 1925: 'Anything I can do to help you get what you can off *those fellows* I will.'[13]

It was in this spirit that Craig went to Dublin in May 1921 — not to submit to de Valera, but to see if the two parts of Ireland could exist in harmony. It was a courageous attempt, but the failure of the meeting meant that partition remained an outstand-ing issue and became the dominant question during the general election. The followers of the old Irish Parliamentary Party issued a flamboyant manifesto condemning partition as a violation of Ireland's 'historic unity' and declaring their 'fixed determina-tion not to enter this North-East Ulster Parliament' if elected. Sinn Féiners were less verbose but equally determined to be done with partition. On the day before the poll de Valera appealed to the 'men and women of North-East Ulster' to vote 'against war with your fellow countrymen. . . . Vote so that there may be an end to boycott and retaliation, to parti-tion, disunity and ruin. . . . Live in history as having created a truly united Irish nation. Orange and Green together can command the future of Ireland. Ireland

one is Ireland peaceful, prosperous and happy.'
Craig's reply was uncompromising. His final election
message urged Unionists:

> Do your duty. Let no-one stand aside. The cause
> is sacred and worthy of every personal sacrifice.
> Rally round me that I may shatter your enemies
> and their hopes of a Republic flag. The Union Jack
> must sweep the polls. Vote early, work late. The
> eyes of our friends throughout the Empire are
> upon us. Let them see that we are as determined
> as they to uphold the cause of Loyalty.[14]

The Union Jack did sweep the polls. Eighty-nine
per cent of the electorate voted, and when the poll
was declared on 27 May it was a triumph for official
Unionism. Every Unionist candidate who stood was
elected. Unionists had expected to win 32 or 36 seats,
but they won 40, the remaining 12 being equally
divided between Nationalists and Sinn Féin. In Co.
Down Craig received 30,000 first preferences,* and
de Valera came second with slightly more than 16,000.
Unionists were jubilant, but the size of their overall
majority of 28 obscured the facts that they had won
only 2 of the 4 Co. Armagh seats and in the disputed
area of Fermanagh and Tyrone 57 per cent of the
electorate had voted against partition and had returned
4 anti-partition candidates.

The new parliament was formally opened by King
George V on 22 June 1921. The visit, planned with
great care down to the last detail of plaiting with red,
white and blue ribbon the straw edging of the stalls
for the royal horses, bore all the marks of Craig's
talents as an impressario, and Craig rather than the

*He was returned unopposed, as were all the other Co. Down candidates,
in 1925, and, with the abolition of PR in 1929, he was returned
unopposed in 1929, 1933 and 1938 for the single-member constituency
of North Down, a seat which he held until his death in 1940.

King and Queen was the centre of attention that day. His wife's diary well captures Craig's ascendancy and the buoyancy of Ulster Unionists:

> The great day . . . The King and Queen have the most wonderful reception. The decorations everywhere are extremely well done and even the little side streets that they will never be within miles of are draped with bunting and flags, and the pavement and lampposts painted red, white and blue, really most touching, as a sign of their loyalty. Imagine Radicals in England thinking they would ever succeed in driving people like that out of the British Empire, or wanting to! . . . The actual opening was the first of the functions. . . . Then followed our big luncheon, J[ames] sitting between Their Majesties. It proves to be a great success. We then all went across to the Ulster Hall, where addresses were presented. . . . After that there was an investiture. The scenes in the Hall were unforgettable, as the people could not contain themselves, and cheered for several minutes, and broke into singing the National Anthem at a moment when it was not on the official programme. They finally left again for the docks, J[ames] and all the official people going with them, after a visit that was nothing but one huge success from first to last. When J[ames] rejoined me at home again, he heaved the biggest sigh of relief imaginable at having got them safely on to the Royal Yacht again, after such a marvellous day without any *contretemps* to either of them. The King said to J[ames] when he was saying goodbye on the yacht, 'I can't tell you how glad I am I came, but you know my entourage were very much against it.' J[ames] replied, 'Sir, you are surrounded by pessimists; we are all optimists over here.'

It had, indeed, been Craig's day, and his wife long cherished the comments of the British press. *The* *Tatler* wondered how he 'will like his new job. . . . Imagine always having to go about with guards and detectives, I hear Sir James's small daughter simply revels in the life, so somebody's pleased at any rate.' The *Daily Chronicle* was more fulsome:

> Sir James Craig had a fine reception when he drove up. He has been an outstanding figure of course in today's ceremonies, and this sketch of him flung at me in a few vivid words by one of his friends, is pertinent. He is a man of character rather than subtlety. He is ready with a plan and goes straight to his object, disregarding cross-currents and side issues. A man of great common sense, he has much of the nature of General Botha. It may be added that he has as difficult a part to play as General Botha, but his friends believe he will succeed.[15]

2

Craig was sorely in need of Botha's qualities, for despite the euphoria of the state opening of parliament, the continued existence of Northern Ireland was by no means assured in 1921−22. His infant administration faced serious challenges within and without. The new regime was boycotted by the Catholic/nationalist minority. Nationalist and Sinn Féin MPs did not take their seats in the new parliament, and twenty-one nationalist-controlled local councils refused to recognise the authority of the new government, as did a large number of Catholic schoolteachers and managers. Moreover, internal tension was further heightened by recurrent violence. Although a truce was signed in July 1921 to end the Anglo-Irish War as a prelude to negotiations between the imperial government and Sinn Féin, it did not bring peace to Northern Ireland.

The IRA consolidated its position there and communal violence continued as Catholics and Protestants fought each other in the cities of Belfast and Londonderry. All too often individuals took the law into their own hands, and defence associations, originally formed among respectable people for self-protection, soon degenerated into murder gangs, such as the Ulster Protestant Association (UPA), which by the autumn of 1921 had turned into an efficiently organised gang of the lowest and least desirable of the Protestant hooligan element, dedicated to the extermination of Catholics.

Uncertainty and tension within Northern Ireland was in part a reflection of uncertainty and tension without. Nationalists in the South had never accepted the validity of partition and continued to dismiss Ulster Unionism as an artificially contrived movement maintained, so Arthur Griffith claimed, by 'a number of men . . . who think that by keeping up the bogey of the Pope and the Boyne they can keep the industrial population quiet'.[16] It is true that Sinn Féin was more interested in Irish independence than Irish unity, but Northern Ireland's status did provide a good bargaining point in discussions with the imperial government. The likelihood that Sinn Féin would stage a break on Ulster made the imperial government reluctant to give Northern Ireland unqualified support. The imperial government regarded partition as the 'worst ground to fight on', for Austen Chamberlain, the Conservative leader and Lord Privy Seal, told his wife: 'You could not raise an army in England to fight for *that* as we could for crown and empire.'[17] This is what happened in the negotiations that eventually led on 6 December 1921 to the signing of the Anglo-Irish Treaty, which superseded the Government of Ireland Act in the South and created the Irish Free State with dominion status. Up until the last minute it had looked as though the position of Northern Ireland would prove a stumbling-block to agreement, and tremendous pressure was put upon Craig by the imperial government and the British press to make concessions to peace by acknowledging the authority not of Westminster but of Dublin.

Such complicated cross-currents posed serious problems for Craig as leader of an inexperienced administration and a movement which had not been educated to accept the responsibilities of government. He had to operate on three separate but interacting fronts — Belfast, Dublin and London, but his response underlined his positive qualities as a leader: energy, courage, fortitude and determination.

It was an uncomfortable existence. His life was in such constant danger that he lived among barbed wire entanglements, bomb-proof netting and armed sentries, but he did not remain immobile or isolated. He frequently braved the uncomfortable journey between Belfast and London to ensure that Northern Ireland's case was understood by his former government and parliamentary colleagues at Westminster; when in Northern Ireland he was always ready to receive deputations and individuals; and he was prepared to venture to Dublin. His moments of relaxation were few, perhaps patience or puzzles, and Lilian Spender, the Cabinet Secretary's wife, liked to switch Craig onto crossword puzzles and 'off politics whenever I get a chance, as they do rest him, & Lady C is much too fond of talking politics *all* through his rest time. He is looking very strained & tired, & no wonder.' [18]

Craig did indeed at times get tired and depressed — and angry. Dealing with Lloyd George, the imperial Prime Minister, was particularly trying, and it was after a round of meetings following the signing of the Treaty that Dixon, the Chief Whip, met Craig in Lon-

don and found him 'depressed for the first time'.
[64] 'Poor dear,' remarked Lady Craig, 'he has had a
dreadful time with all these twisters to deal with. . . .
It is sickening the way he has been treated, after all
his work and honest dealing, and makes one fed up
with politics.' Nor were Craig's efforts always appreciated by his so-called followers in Northern Ireland,
causing his wife to expostulate:

> What makes me so raging is the lack of guts of
> them all, none of the people who really heartily
> approve of his action have the courage to get up
> and say so. . . . It makes one wonder whether they
> are worth someone slaving themselves almost to
> death for.[19]

Yet Craig did not allow himself to be overwhelmed
by depression. Nor did he allow anger to dictate his
policy. He continued to slave away to preserve
Northern Ireland and tried to do so by conciliation
rather than coercion and confrontation. Between
June and December 1921 he operated mainly in
Britain. After the fiasco of his meeting with de
Valera the previous May he saw no point in further
contacts with the South, especially since his supporters were convinced that Southern leaders were
nothing but traitors and murderers. Moreover, de
Valera had managed to offend the normally placid
Craig. On being invited to meet Lloyd George in
London to discuss an Irish settlement, de Valera,
representing himself as spokesman for the whole
nation properly sounding out one of the minority
leaders, asked Craig to go to Dublin for consultations.
This Craig considered sheer insolence. He was, after
all, Prime Minister of Northern Ireland, a government
constitutionally established by act of parliament.

Nor was there much for Craig to do in Northern
Ireland, since very few powers were transferred from

Westminster in 1921. The energies he did spare for internal affairs he devoted to trying to calm the fears of his supporters on the almost intractable problem of law and order. Many appeals were addressed to Craig by Unionists for protection not only from nationalist but also from loyalist violence. Perhaps the most pathetic yet dignified of these appeals came in September 1921 from a sixty-year old 'staunch Unionist' who had been 'brought up in the Army as a lad in India' and had always loved the British Empire. He had, however, married a Catholic wife, 'whom I still have the highest respect for', and had four daughters and two sons, the latter living away from home. Describing 'the present deplorable condition of East Belfast, as it affects myself personally', Craig's correspondent related how on the evening of 24 September 1921 four hooligans (probably members of the UPA), 'smelling of strong drink' and using language 'unspeakable in the presence of my wife', came to the house to demand one of his sons who had recently been at home but was then working away. Thereupon 'they ordered me to leave the house within a week & showed me some bullets, and said I "would get one of them thro' me if I didn't leave" as "it was orders from Head Quarters". And we may be wrecked and looted and maltreated at any moment day or night.' Craig's correspondent was particularly indignant that the

> fact of my being a Unionist & Loyalist did not count. . . . Clearly it is not a question of Sinn Féin against Loyalist, but purely one of ignorant bigotry. . . . To think that Loyalty should be subjected to such worry & strain at the hands of *so-called* Loyalists is enough to make one despair of Civilisation & Christianity ever coming to maturity . . . for so far both influences seem a failure.[20]

Yet conscious though he was of the need to curb
[66] impending anarchy, Craig's hands were tied by the
fact that the maintenance of law and order remained
the responsibility of Westminster. All he could do
was, on the one hand, to appeal to the imperial
authorities to act more decisively by applying their
powers under the Restoration of Order in Ireland Act
and making full use of the Special Constabulary; and,
on the other, to try to assuage the fears of his supporters and persuade them not to take the law into
their own hands. Thus, following attacks on men
going to and from the shipyards, Craig was at pains to
dissuade Protestant ex-servicemen employed there
from organising for self-protection. The mastermind
of the UVF of 1912–14, Craig knew all about the
difficulties and dangers of irregular forces, and in
September 1921 he urged a deputation from the ex-
servicemen that 'Nobody in the present circumstances
could undertake the protection of citizens except the
State.' To form vigilante groups, he warned, would
only play into the hands of Northern Ireland's
enemies. Instead Craig tried to channel these energies
more constructively by proposing that the deputation
should form 'a special Watch Committee', which
might 'come and tell him what they thought was
wrong'.[21]

Craig's main concern was not with events in the
South or in the North but with events in Britain. It
was at Westminster that the battle for Northern
Ireland's survival could be most obviously won or
lost. Westminster could determine Northern Ireland's
legal status and position within the United Kingdom,
and provide, or withhold, the money and materials
necessary for survival. Thus in 1921 and in the following year Craig spent an increasing amount of time in
London and had often to be kept informed of events
in Northern Ireland by means of letters and telegrams

from his cabinet secretariat. There were obvious disadvantages in such a remote form of leadership, but, as Craig explained during one set of negotiations between Westminster and Dublin, 'I am inclined to believe that I am of more service here at the moment,' for after every meeting between imperial and Southern leaders 'it is necessary for me to supply a "corrective", otherwise action on our behalf is delayed. I have been doing this work five times during last week and this with, what I believe to be, good results.'[22]

Only Craig among the Ulster Unionists could have fulfilled this role. He personally knew many members of the imperial government, and his equable temperament enabled him to discuss the most sensitive issues with the minimum of rancour and drama. Imperial ministers and officials found Craig very different from the Southern Irish to deal with. 'There is an anthracite quality about these Ulstermen,' commented one Colonial Office official after a long meeting with Craig, 'very unlike the Southern Irish tinder which blazes up the moment the spark falls.'[23] Such phlegmatism may have disconcerted those with whom he had to negotiate, but it was a source of comfort and even joy to his own colleagues and officials. The Northern Ireland Cabinet Secretary, Wilfrid Spender, an unimpressionable Englishman, much admired Craig's 'clear head, his grasp of essentials, his moderation, & his bland indifference to the big guns the British Cabinet bring to bear upon him', and used to sit by and chortle as he watched Craig 'being ponderously playful when he ought to be overawed, & invincibly cheerful when L[loyd] G[eorge] turns on the pathetic tap'.[24]

In 1921 Craig's preoccupation was the defence of Northern Ireland's position during the negotiations that led up to the Anglo-Irish Treaty. How this could best be done was a matter of some debate. Lloyd

George did invite Craig to take part in tripartite talks with himself and de Valera, but the invitation was declined, since Craig took the view that it was up to de Valera and the imperial government to come to terms on the question of self-determination for the twenty-six counties. Northern Ireland had already determined its own future. All he would do was to promise co-operation on equal terms with the South on any matters affecting their common interests.

This attitude was a logical one, but it did make difficult the defence of Northern Ireland's interests when partition became a crucial issue during the negotiations and the imperial government was inclined to surrender to Dublin control over the North. Arriving at the Savoy Hotel in London at the beginning of November 1921, 'as jolly as a sandlark, looking forward to our week-end' with his sons, Craig was unexpectedly summoned to a meeting with Lloyd George who asked him to make concessions for the sake of a settlement. In view of the pledges made in 1914—20, it was, Craig later told his wife, 'the biggest shock he has ever had in his life, at finding so many "backsliders" amongst his old friends and colleagues'. His response was, however, a masterly one — firm but polite. He flatly refused to have anything to do with the proposal to exchange Westminster's sovereignty over the six counties for that of Dublin. He demanded a precise timetable for the transfer of services to Northern Ireland, in order to consolidate its position. And he remained impervious to Lloyd George's threats of resignation. When Lloyd George remarked: 'This may be a most historical meeting, as I may be forced to resign,' Craig unsympathetically replied: 'Is it not wonderful how many great men have come to grief over the eternal Irish question?'[25]

Craig also got the better of Lloyd George in a subsequent exchange of letters, in which the latter tried to induce Northern Ireland to accept the authority of a Dublin parliament. It was probably for this reason as much as the serious bout of influenza which then afflicted Craig that he was henceforth kept in the dark about the progress of the negotiations and the way in which the negotiators were working towards a compromise on the Ulster question. He was shown the final terms of the Anglo-Irish Treaty only hours before their publication on 6 December 1921. A new Irish government and parliament, the Irish Free State, was to have authority over the whole of Ireland, but Northern Ireland was given the right to opt out and retain its position and status within the United Kingdom. In the inevitable event of Northern Ireland opting out, article 12 of the Treaty provided for the appointment of a Boundary Commission to revise the border between the two areas.

The terms of the Treaty and their implications for Northern Ireland came as a bitter shock to Craig. In some respects the Treaty represented a reward for his stubborn resistance to the cajoling and threats of Lloyd George and the British press. Craig had become the unseen dominating force in the negotiations, and thus the Treaty had perforce to make provision for the continued existence of Northern Ireland within the United Kingdom. Craig was, however, more concerned with the general tenor of the agreement, which he regarded as a blatant violation of the previous pledges he and Ulster Unionists had been given by the imperial government. His feeling of betrayal permeated the dignified letter of protest he sent on behalf of his government to Lloyd George on 14 December 1921. The declared intention to place Northern Ireland automatically in the Irish Free State, despite the right to opt out, 'is a complete reversal' of the declared imperial policy' that 'Ulster should remain out until she chose of her free will to enter an all-

Ireland Parliament'. Such an 'astounding change'
represented 'a surrender to the claims of *Sinn Féin*
that her delegates must be recognised as the representatives of the whole of Ireland — a claim which we
cannot for a moment admit'. As for the proposal for
a Boundary Commission, not only was it a breach of
the 1920 act, but there was 'no precedent in the history of the British Empire for taking any territory
from an established Government without its sanction'.
Craig therefore 'reserved to my Government the right
of dissenting from the appointment of any boundary
commission'. It was in this letter that Craig anticipated
the value of Northern Ireland's ports to the Empire
during the Second World War, prohesying that 'In
years to come the British nation will realise the
advantages in having in Northern Ireland a population
which is determined to remain loyal to British traditions and citizenship.'[26]

3

Craig was right to be angry at the terms of the Treaty.
Article 12 may have been a master-stroke in prevent-
ing the Treaty negotiations breaking down on the
Ulster question, but it served only to intensify the
problems facing Northern Ireland. It heightened
apprehensions among Unionists, particularly those
living in border areas, who were alarmed at the possibility of being transferred to the Free State. It also
created among nationalists in the North and South an
expectation that Northern Ireland would soon dis-
appear and a notion that its territory was a legitimate
target for seizure.

The difficulties created in the North by the Treaty
were further accentuated by a split in the South over
its terms. The supporters of the Treaty, largely led by
Michael Collins, formed a Provisional Government,

but critics, led by de Valera, took an increasingly hostile stance culminating in a civil war. The IRA, which had never ceased to operate in the North, received a new impetus from the split, as supporters and opponents of the Treaty among its members co-operated in a campaign against the North and the Northern divisions of the IRA were reorganised and armed by Collins so that they might protect the Northern minority and prevent the Northern government from establishing control. In 1922, therefore, Northern Ireland was faced with a double security problem. Law and order had to be maintained within (a complicated enough task involving resistance to subversion and keeping Protestant and Catholic apart), and the long and tortuous border had to be secured against attack from without.

Tension along the border was brought almost to fever pitch by such dramatic incidents as the kidnapping of loyalists who were then held as hostages south of the border in February 1922 and the occupation in the following May of Northern territory by the IRA. Indeed, the brief occupation by the IRA of one village had, it was reported six months later, 'reduced the local Unionists to a state of nerves, comparable only . . . to the panic among the better class of inhabitants of villages which the Bolsheviks have once held and threaten to revisit'.[27] Internally, there were incidents in most parts of the six counties, but the main trouble-spot was Belfast, where bombing, arson, intimidation, expulsion from home and work, and murder became a part of life. Such violence reached its peak in the second and third weeks of May 1922, when a renewed IRA assault provoked fierce Protestant retaliation.

This violence, resulting as it did in the death of more Catholics than Protestants, reacted upon the external situation. Events in the North were used by opponents of the Treaty in the South to assail the

Provisional Government there. Collins took an intense [72] personal, even hysterical, interest in the treatment of the Northern minority, and, since as a poor judge of character he never trusted Craig, whom he once described as 'a wily bird',[28] he was constantly appealing to the imperial government that the extermination of Northern Catholics, as he put it, was undermining his position and thus the Treaty in the South. Such representations seriously worried the imperial government lest it should become tarred with the same brush as Ulster Unionism and the South be given an excuse to renege on the Treaty. This attitude in turn reacted upon the North, since by 1922 Northern Ireland was beginning to assume responsibility for many services, including law and order, but continued to require British co-operation and cash to operate these services. Thus once again, in 1922 as in 1921, great pressure was brought to bear on Craig and the government of Northern Ireland, not to enter a Dublin parliament but to mend their ways and so, Lloyd George hoped, 'eliminate the Ulster issue and leave a clean issue of "Republic versus British Empire"'.[29]

Not surprisingly, therefore, Craig continued to be preoccupied by dealings with Westminster. This time his task was to ensure that the imperial government would allow Northern Ireland sufficient resources to maintain a civilised existence. Expenditure was much higher than had been anticipated when the 1920 act had been drafted. The cost of unemployment insurance and of maintaining law and order was high, and the fact that Northern Ireland's contribution to imperial services was a first, fixed and exorbitant charge on its revenue meant that Northern Ireland faced budget deficits during the first two financial years. Craig therefore began to press the imperial government not only for special grants towards the cost of unemployment insurance and the Special Constabulary but also for a revision of the financial provisions of the 1920 act.

This was no easy task, for these financial claims were met with some hostility by the Treasury, which thought that Northern Ireland should stand on its own financial feet and should not sponge off the British taxpayer. Senior Treasury officials particularly disliked Craig's informal methods of conducting business and his demand that the imperial government should spend millions of pounds on the Special Constabulary, over which it had no control. 'Sir James Craig', the Deputy Controller of Finance remarked to the Chancellor of the Exchequer on 24 May 1922, 'rather humorously says that the last thing in his mind is to escape the obligations of the 1920 Act. But under the Act the *whole* obligation for Specials is on the Ulster Exchequer!'[30] Appalled though the Treasury was by Craig's insistence on *ad hoc* payments, it was even more taken aback when, in November 1922, Craig presented detailed proposals for a revision of the financial relations between Britain and Northern Ireland. 'Incredible if they were not in black and white,' expostulated the Deputy Controller.[31]

Moreover, there was a general feeling among ministers and civil servants in Britain that Northern Ireland did not necessarily merit assistance, since events there were in danger of upsetting the Treaty in the South. In particular, there were grave doubts about the wisdom of financing the Special Constabulary, the very people whom the Provisional Government was accusing of exterminating Catholics. Among imperial ministers, only Winston Churchill, the Colonial Secretary and minister responsible for Irish affairs, and, to a lesser extent, Arthur Balfour, the Conservative Lord President of the Council, appreciated that Northern Ireland's special problems merited sympa-

thetic handling. What is more, such feelings of resent-
[74] ment and suspicion were heartily reciprocated by
Ulster Unionists within and without the government.
They believed that Westminster was far too responsive
to the lying propaganda of the South. 'I declare,' Craig
told MPs, 'if a cow died in Kerry they would say it
was Belfast or Ulster was the cause of it.'[32]

Although feelings were running high in 1922, Craig's
dealings with the imperial government continued to
be characterised by firmness and tact. He cultivated
friendly relations with Churchill and was always willing to talk to imperial ministers and officials on any
matter affecting the peace of Ireland, not simply to
put the North's viewpoint but also to learn the views
of others.

It was this willingness to learn and be guided by
others that led him to accept Churchill's suggestion
that he should try once more to reach agreement with
the South, or rather with those Southern leaders who
had signed the Treaty and had formed the Provisional
Government. Accordingly on 24 January 1922 he
met Collins in London to see if agreement could be
reached on the border. During a three-hour meeting
Craig asked Collins 'straight out whether it was his
intention to have peace in Ireland or whether we were
to go on with murder and strife, rivalry and boycott
and unrest in Northern Ireland'. It was a hopeful
meeting for, according to Craig, Collins 'made it clear
that he wanted a real peace and that he had so many
troubles in Southern Ireland, that he was prepared to
establish cordial relations with Northern Ireland, and
to abandon all attempts to coercion, but hoping to
coax her into a union later'.[33] In particular, it was
decided to dispense with the dreaded Boundary Commission and to settle the question of the border directly
between the two Irish governments. Craig's optimism
quickly evaporated when on 2 February he and the

Cabinet Secretary, Spender, visited Dublin to iron out the details of a border settlement. It transpired that the January accord had been based upon a misunderstanding. Craig had been assured by Lloyd George that only minor rectifications of the boundary had been contemplated, but Collins and the other Irish negotiators had been led to expect that substantial tracts of Northern Ireland would be transferred to the South. Craig's disappointment was reflected in Spender's remarks to his wife: 'It seems as if Collins had found the extreme elements in S. Ireland too much for him, & had to give way to them — in other words, that he is afraid of them, for officials in Dublin declare that if he came out strongly for law & order, & stable Govt, he could undoubtedly rally the majority of the people to him.'[34]

Craig's disappointment turned to burning anger after the border raids and he alarmed the imperial cabinet by his proposals for securing the release of the kidnapped loyalists. Austen Chamberlain, the Conservative leader and Lloyd George's second-in-command, reported that unless the kidnapped men were quickly released, Craig would

> arrest a similar number of known and 'poisonous' Sinn Féiners resident in the North: that he should conduct them under guard to a place on the boundary, and then tell them to go into the South to argue and reason with the Sinn Féiners of the South for the release of the captives, and that he should warn them that unless they could secure the release of these men unharmed, they were not to recross the boundary, and that if they did so it would be at their own peril. If this did not secure their release, he would later seize a further batch of Northern Sinn Féiners and treat them in the same way, and so on. In this manner, if he did not get

back his own people, he would at least get rid of a number of poisonous Sinn Féiners.[35]

Yet Craig realised that wrath was no basis for policy and that it was not in Northern Ireland's interests to allow a complete rift with the South. Thus it was that he responded at the end of March to Churchill's appeals for a further meeting in London with Collins. He did so against the wishes of colleagues, officials and supporters, as the loathing they felt for the South had developed to such a pitch that Spender, who again accompanied Craig, so positioned himself that he did not have to shake hands with the Southern delegation. In fact he was appalled by the attitude adopted by Collins, who, looking like 'the hero of an American film drama'[36] and in a truculently boastful mood, made no attempt to deny responsibility for outrages in the North and even claimed absolute control over the activities of the IRA. Craig was more willing to make allowances for Collins's internal difficulties, and the upshot of prolonged discussions was another abortive agreement, the peace pact of 30 March 1922, the first clause of which ran 'PEACE is today declared.'[37]

Peace did not last long, and relations between North and South broke down completely after the electoral pact between Collins and de Valera in the following May. Craig was outraged by this agreement, which he regarded as the prelude to a concerted attack on the North, especially since it coincided with renewed IRA violence. He could scarcely restrain his emotions and spoke out in his most defiant vein. 'There is a complete washout,' he told the House of Commons. ' . . . We will hear no more about a Commission coming to decide whether our boundaries shall be so and so. What we have now we hold, and we will hold against all combinations.'[38] It was a hard-hitting speech, which brought from Churchill a private scold, accusing Craig of ingratitude and pro- vocation. Yet it reflected Craig's disgust with the South, and it was not until after the more moderate William Cosgrave took over the Provisional Government after Collins's assassination the following August that Craig was once again prepared to consider trimming policies to suit the South.

The fact that agreements with Collins proved so abortive inevitably raises the question as to whether Craig should ever have attempted to come to terms with the South in the first place. Consultations with Southern leaders served only to strengthen the position of the more uncompromising among Northern nationalists and raised false hopes in others. Talk about the return of Catholics expelled from the ship-yards or their homes was unrealistic at a time of high unemployment and a housing shortage, and merely provided occasion for future recriminations when expectations were not realised. On the other hand, Unionist fears and resentments were increased. Such proposals as the numbering and disarming of the police seemed simply to invite identification and assassination. Yet the fact that he risked the hostility of his own supporters and the dangers of visiting Dublin was a tribute to Craig's courage and determination to achieve peace. As he told his wife prior to the January meeting with Collins, 'No stone ought to be left unturned to try and stop the murdering that is going on in Ireland.'[39] And, as he told one correspondent after the signing of the peace pact,

The question is so big that I have determined to pursue a steady straight course and to pay as little attention as possible to those critics who — though well-meaning — have not yet been trained in a wider outlook.[40]

Moreover, Craig's willingness to meet members of [78] the Provisional Government eased the course of his dealings with the imperial government, where his determination to pursue 'a steady straight course' was most clearly in evidence. Throughout he was concerned not to score points but to settle outstanding problems amicably and fairly. He was ever ready to argue a reasoned case for British assistance in balancing the budget and maintaining law and order. He held that Ulster Unionists had not sought a government of their own and had accepted one only to assist the imperial government to resolve the Irish question; that the imperial government had handed Northern Ireland over in a deplorable and disorderly condition with an uneasy neighbour to the South; and that, anyway, despite the existence of a regional government, Northern Ireland remained an integral part of the United Kingdom. Therefore the imperial government was morally and even legally obliged to repair the damage and help maintain Northern Ireland. As Craig told Churchill on 26 May 1922, 'In helping us in the generous way you are doing you are only carrying out British traditions. . . . In coming to our rescue — as you put it — you are only doing what would be done if one of the eastern counties was threatened by an enemy from without.'[41]

How well Craig steered the difficult course between conflicting imperial and Northern Ireland perspectives was illustrated by his avoidance of a constitutional crisis over the Local Government Bill in the summer of 1922. This bill abolished PR in local elections, which since its introduction in 1919 had resulted in substantial Unionist losses, particularly to nationalists, who in the 1920 local elections had gained clear majorities in such traditionally marginal authorities as the Fermanagh and Tyrone County Councils and Londonderry Corporation. The Local Government

Bill was, therefore, a prompt response to the demands of local Unionist organisations, anxious to regain the ground lost in 1920. In the absence of nationalist MPs, the bill speedily completed an unopposed parliamentary progress on 5 July 1922, but the royal assent was withheld until the following September. The delay was the result of the Provisional Government's opposition to the bill as unfair to the minority and a violation of the Treaty. The withholding of the assent at the behest of the Provisional Government almost precipitated a constitutional crisis. Ministers and senior officials in Northern Ireland were incensed by what they regarded as yet another example of the intolerable treatment meted out to Northern Ireland by the imperial authorities. They wanted to bring about a showdown with the imperial government by resigning and holding a general election.

Craig sympathised with such indignation. He too was much exercised by the principle of withholding the royal assent from a bill which was clearly within the competence of the parliament of Northern Ireland and had been approved by an overwhelming majority of the electorate. Should the royal assent not be given to such a measure, then his government would have no alternative but to resign. 'No Government could carry on in Northern Ireland', he told the Permanent Secretary of the Colonial Office on 22 July 1922, 'if it knew that the powers of the Parliament . . . were to be abrogated.'[42] The creation of such a precedent would warrant the interference of the imperial government in almost every bill introduced in Northern Ireland.

Unlike his colleagues, however, Craig was in no hurry to precipitate a showdown. In the first place, he thought that dramatic gestures were unnecessary, since he believed that the imperial government would back down rather than run 'the risk of complete dis-

organisation in Ulster at the moment'.[43] He was right.
[80] The imperial government did quail before the prospect
of Craig's resignation over the Local Government
Bill. Resignation would have meant a general election
in Northern Ireland, which, in view of the built-in
Unionist majority and the widespread Unionist dislike of PR, would have endorsed Craig's action. The
imperial government would have been obliged either
to climb down or to resume responsibility for govern-
ing the province — the very thing the 1920 act had
been designed to avoid. Moreover, Craig did not think
that a conflict with the imperial government was in
Northern Ireland's best interests. Sentiment apart,
he knew how much it relied upon imperial financial
and other help. At the very time when his minsters
were pressing for confrontation, he was in England
discussing with the imperial ministers the future
financing of the Special Constabulary, and he did not
want this question linked with that of the Local
Government Bill.

Thus, although he would not budge on the main
question and stood by the bill, Craig maintained a
conciliatory attitude. He damped down all public
reference in Northern Ireland to the question of the
withholding of the royal assent. He willingly discussed
at length the implications of the bill with Churchill
and his officials and took in good part their little
lectures on the need to take a broad view of affairs
and the importance of winning over the Northern
minority. Finally, he made two minor concessions
which enabled a crisis to be averted and allowed the
imperial government to retreat gracefully while offer-
ing a sop to the Provisional Government in the South.

4

Masterly though his handling of this episode was as an
exercise in external diplomacy, the bill itself was a

blunder from the point of view of internal politics and revealed those two fatal flaws of leadership which were to mar Craig's subsequent career as premier. The first flaw was his inability to assess the broad and long-term effects of actions and relate different aspects of policy to a broader strategy of government. The second was his inability or unwillingness to impose his views upon his followers and to supervise the implementation of policies he had helped to conceive, or, to put it less charitably, the ease with which he could be overborne by the more uncompromising members of his party and administration.

Thus his sole concern with the Local Government Bill was to give effect to the views of the Unionist rank and file agitating for the abolition of PR. There was no consideration of the wider implications of abolition, particularly in respect of minorities and the attempt he was making to persuade certain Belfast Catholics to recognise his government. For some time Craig had been trying to associate Catholics with his regime. Despite protests from loyalist organisations, he seemed determined in 1921–22 to recruit civil servants from all sections of the community, provided only that they were loyal to the government, and he accepted a recommendation of a parliamentary committee that Catholics should comprise one-third of the newly formed Royal Ulster Constabulary (RUC). Eventually, too, Craig was brought into direct contact with certain Belfast Catholics, who reported to the local bishop. The minority in Belfast was divided into supporters of the old Irish Parliamentary Party (now generally known in Northern Ireland as Nationalists) and those of the more uncompromising Sinn Féin or Republican party. The former were the stronger, but Sinn Féin's ascendancy in the rest of Ireland, and the interest taken by Collins in the fate of the Northern minority, not only enhanced the prestige of Sinn Féin in Belfast, but also made it [82] dangerous for Catholics and nationalists to declare openly for Craig's government. Some concessions were necessary to ease the path of the constitutionalists, and therefore from March 1922 onwards Craig and the Cabinet Secretary, Spender, discussed with such prominent Catholics as Raymond Burke, a wealthy Belfast shipbroker, the terms, particularly in relation to education, upon which they would be ready to co-operate with the government. Even though they might not lead to formal Catholic recognition, Craig believed that such close contacts with a man such as Burke were useful, if only because 'it will make it more difficult for him to be antagonistic in the future'.[44]

By the early summer of 1922 there were good grounds for believing, as Spender reported to Craig on 14 June 1922, between the first and second readings of the Local Government Bill, that 'Collins was losing ground daily in Northern Ireland'.[45] But Craig did not seem to realise that this process of reconciliation might be hindered by the abolition of PR, which would not only upset the Northern minority but would also give Collins an opportunity to reassert himself in the North. Only after Collins's intervention at Westminster did it dawn on Craig that there was more to PR than the satisfaction of Unionist demands for its abolition. Even then realisation was tinged with disbelief and the whole episode really did underline Craig's unfortunate tendency to keep, as one senior Colonial Office official put it, 'several watertight compartments in his mind'.[46]

The same defects of leadership were evident in Craig's handling of the question of law and order, which continued to be the most important internal issue in 1922 as in 1921. In 1922, though, there was a difference, for by then law and order had become a transferred service, the responsibility no longer of

Westminster but of Northern Ireland. Craig fully understood the vital importance of restoring and maintaining law and order, but, although his government did eventually establish control, he signally failed in these crucial early months of responsibility to establish a system of justice which had the confidence of all sections of the community. The system that did emerge gave primacy to narrow policing considerations, tended to discriminate in favour of Protestants and Unionists, and was largely rejected by Catholics and nationalists.

Such developments were not the result of vindictiveness or lack of humanity on Craig's part. His heart was in the right place, and he did want to do right by everybody by combining firmness with justice and compassion. He really did hope to order Northern Ireland's internal affairs on the basis of conciliation rather than coercion. Nor does the existence of the Civil Authorities (Special Powers) Act, hurriedly passed in the spring of 1922, and Craig's faith in the Ulster Special Constabulary contradict this proposition. A degree of force was necessary, but law enforcement was not as severe and brutal as hostile critics of Northern Ireland have liked to suggest. Craig had no alternative but to rely upon the almost exclusively Protestant Special Constabulary as the main peacekeeping agency in 1922 in view of the imperial government's determination to disband the Royal Irish Constabulary and its reluctance to use the army as a police force in Northern Ireland. The Special Powers Act was a legitimate response to the problem of maintaining law and order. It had been urged on Craig by the army, which was loath to use its powers under the Restoration of Order in Ireland Act; it was less far-reaching than the British act — and subsequent anti-terrorist laws in the South; and Craig only reluctantly authorised the use of the new powers.

The problem was that Craig could not think through [84] the implications of policies on law and order or force policies on unwilling colleagues and supporters. The first failure was evident in his invitation to Field-Marshal Sir Henry Wilson to advise him on security matters and in the consequent appointment of an English officer, Major-General A. Solly-Flood, as Military Adviser. It was certainly a dramatic and prompt response to IRA border raids, but it created more bother than benefit. Not only did it give rise to adverse publicity in the South and in Britain, but it also created problems among Ulster Unionists and with the imperial government, as Solly-Flood's efforts to reorganise the Special Constabulary and create in effect a territorial army, complete with tanks and planes, had to be restrained by Craig and the Colonial and War Offices.

The second defect of his leadership — failure to see policies through — was equally unfortunate and ultimately disastrous to Northern Ireland. In view of the often violent feelings of his followers and colleagues, it was no easy task to implement policies of conciliation, and Craig did make some effort to educate Unionists to take a broad and calm view of events. In the furore following the announcement of the Treaty, he preached restraint, urging MPs that 'We should hold our hand . . . and show that moderation which has always characterised us when any crisis has to be faced.'[47] After his first meeting with Collins, in January 1922, he tried to persuade Protestant shipyard workers to allow expelled Catholics to return to the yards, pointing out that not all Catholics were traitors or gunmen, but simply men with livings to earn. He also tried to prevent his cabinet colleagues from reacting hastily to events, particularly Collins's continued denunciations of the North after the peace pact of 30 March. Such denunciations sorely tried the patience of ministers and officials, but Craig was quick to remind them of the difficulties facing the Provisional Government in the South. Thus after one of Collins's more outlandish outbursts Craig told the Cabinet Secretary that it would be judicious to say nothing in reply, since Collins had 'either been unnecessarily impetuous or endeavoured to curry favour with his own extreme faction'.[48]

The trouble was that in the last analysis Craig was unwilling to force his views either on his followers or, more culpably, on the ministers he was supposed to lead. Such a failure to do so ruined what little chance of success the peace pact of March 1922 had of establishing harmony in Northern Ireland. Having signed the pact in London, Craig was largely content to leave its implementation to his ministers. This delegation was justified in relation to the Minister of Labour, Andrews, who showed patience and tact in securing the co-operation of Collins and Catholics in the administration of the unemployment grant provided by the imperial government under clause 9 of the pact. Less happy was Bates's handling of the controversial provisions relating to law and order. It is true that the agreement did raise the vexed question of the propriety of executive interference in the due processes of law, and that the attitude of Collins and a section of the Northern minority hardly encouraged co-operation in such sensitive matters. Yet the root of the trouble was that the pact was unpopular with the military and police authorities, and that ministers and officials connected with the administration of law and order showed no urgency, imagination or generosity in implementing it. On the contrary, the Junior Minister of Home Affairs and the Attorney-General both threatened to resign, and at this time the Ministry of Home Affairs showed a contemptuous rather than an accommodating attitude to the mino-

rity. Although Bates expected 'the better RC element
[86] to break off from S[inn] F[éin]', [49] his ministry
showed scant courtesy to those Catholics who visited
it, making them wait in outer offices for hours on
end. All this was going on while Craig was in London,
trying to sort out Northern Ireland's finances instead
of supervising the implementation of the pact in Belfast. There was a sad contrast between the generosity
of his intentions and the hostile spirit in which the
Ministry of Home Affairs acted.

It was the same story on most matters relating to
the administration of law and order in 1922. Craig
allowed his own views on what was right and proper
to be overruled by the Ministry of Home Affairs.
Thus, despite his conviction of the need for stern
disciplinary action, Bates's fear of upsetting Belfast
Orangemen allowed a particularly partisan and in-
subordinate officer in the RUC, J. W. Nixon, later
an Independent Unionist MP, to continue to rule the
roost in his district, despite showing, Bates told Craig
on 23 October 1922, 'strong party feeling which is
unbecoming in a police officer' and allowing to
develop there the feeling that 'there is only one law
and that for the Protestants, and in consequence the
Protestant hooligan is allowed to interpret in his own
fashion the laws of the country'.[50] Similarly, there
were good reasons for remitting flogging sentences on
nationalists in order to oblige both Churchill, from
whom Craig had 'a good many favours to secure', and
Cosgrave, the new leader of the Provisional Government in the South, whom Churchill reckoned would
be 'more reasonable to deal with than Collins'.[51] Yet
Craig refused to act against the advice of the Ministry
of Home Affairs, which vehemently opposed remis-
sion on the grounds that any political interference
with due judicial processes would undermine all
attempts to establish and maintain law and order

in Northern Ireland. The principles applicable to flogging cases were, Megaw, the Junior Minister of Home
Affairs, insisted, 'in general those affecting ordinary
administration of law and order. Is the law to be firmly
administered, or is its administration to be dependent
on agitation or pressure from within or without?'[52]

This was a fine sentiment, and would have been
even finer had it been applied consistently. The
trouble was that the Ministry of Home Affairs and
the police authorities were inclined to apply the law
and special powers strictly against Catholics and
nationalists, but more circumspectly in relation to
Protestants and Unionists. There was even, Spender
reported to Craig on 1 August 1922, a widely held
view in the Ministry of Home Affairs that 'the law
does not matter when dealing with suspected treason-
able criminals'.[53] Yet Craig did nothing to correct
this tendency and even tolerated attempts to tame
the toughs of the UPA by enrolling them in the Special
Constabulary and enlisting their aid in the work of
a newly established Secret Service. When this attempt
failed and they resumed their attacks on Catholics,
Craig accepted the Military Adviser's explanation as
to why special powers should not be used to crush
the gang. According to Solly-Flood, 'Any drastic
action in loyal areas for the sake of punishing a few
rogues might incite an outbreak of outrages on a
large scale.'[54]

Craig, indeed, almost abandoned any responsibility
for the administration of law and order, which he
thought should be left in the hands of the appropriate
authorities. As he told the Cabinet Secretary on 10
June 1922, 'I am particularly anxious not to get into
the position that Catholics always come squealing to
me when hit hard by Solly Flood.'[55]

[88] Although significant for the future, Craig's deficiencies as a leader — his shortsightedness and inability to see policies through — were in 1921—22 far outweighed by his positive qualities. His calmness, determination and courage steered Northern Ireland through the violent trauma of its birth. It was because of these qualities that the forces of law and order in Northern Ireland were adequately financed and equipped to resist the IRA onslaught and to contain communal violence, for the imperial Treasury did agree to bear the cost of the Special Constabulary, at that time the main police force. It was because of his perseverance and even insensitivity that Northern Ireland's finances were put on a firmer footing, since the imperial government agreed after much badgering to submit the question to an arbitration committee. The resultant Colwyn Award — a spendthrift's charter, according to the Treasury — made domestic expenditure instead of the crippling imperial contribution the first charge on Northern Ireland's revenue. Admittedly, the threat of the Boundary Commission remained, but by the end of 1922 peace had been established in Northern Ireland, which on 7 December confirmed its status within the United Kingdom by submitting a petition to King George V, formally opting out of the Irish Free State. As Craig said in moving this humble address,

> We . . . feel safe and sure whilst we remain under the Imperial Parliament. . . . We have our right there, we have our say there on those affairs which affect the country and the Empire as a whole, and we have our own institution here with our Senate and our Commons, and I pray God as long as I have anything to do with it we shall remain steadfast in the true faith.[56]

4
Failure

It may seem harsh to label as a failure a man who remained premier for almost twenty years. Yet a failure Craig ultimately was. He had shown both strengths and limitations as a leader in the critical period 1921–22, but after 1922 the latter became the more pronounced, and Craig's subsequent career was a sad anticlimax. An effective leader in a crisis, he did not rise to the challenge posed by the ordinary work of government. It is true that Northern Ireland presented some particularly intractable problems, but it is also true that Craig made no sustained attempt to overcome them and even accentuated some of the difficulties. Such a failure of leadership helps to explain why during his premiership Northern Ireland became not a half-way house sheltering a united and contented people but a ramshackle lean-to rejected by one-third of the population.

1

Admittedly, Craig's was an unenviable task. He emerged from the traumatic violence of the early months only to be faced with dissension and decay. Northern Ireland was by no means an easy or satisfying place to govern in the inter-war years. An ill-conceived structure of government, an ailing economy and a divided society not only posed daunting difficulties, but also prevented their solution. There was little scope for prompt, enterprising or even impartial [90] government.

Craig's government, the regional government, had formal responsibility for a wide range of matters, such as law and order, local government, representation, education, social services, agriculture, industry and internal trade. But it had little real power. Although the executive was unshackled by the cipher of a regional parliament, its freedom of action was severely circumscribed by the fact that it was uncomfortably sandwiched between the imperial government with its exacting Treasury and congeries of parsimonious local authorities, neither of which had a consistent interest in the development of regional policies.

Northern Ireland's seventy-odd local authorities had long been distinguished for their partisanship and lack of dynamism, yet they were responsible for the administration of most of the services transferred to Northern Ireland. They thus came into frequent conflict with the regional government, particularly over the division of financial responsibilities. Northern Ireland's links with Westminster also hindered regional planning. Not only was ultimate sovereignty reserved to Westminster, but so also was a wide range of powers, such as customs and excise and income tax and surtax, affecting economic and social development. Thus, despite the needs of industry and agriculture, the regional government could not impose any form of import control, nor could it regulate its revenue, which was largely determined by Westminster. So debilitating were these financial arrangements that, except for a few years in the 1920s, the government of Northern Ireland was in constant dread of a budget deficit and had to go cap in hand to the imperial Treasury.

The nature of the economy also posed problems.

Northern Ireland did not constitute a separate economy, but rather was the most disadvantaged part of a single economic system embracing the whole United Kingdom. This meant that economic and social problems were relatively more serious in Northern Ireland than in Britain. It also meant that the regional government could take few steps to regenerate the economic life of the province and develop a distinctive economic and social policy to remedy the consequences of Northern Ireland's traditional dependence on a narrow range of now ailing occupations — agriculture, shipbuilding and linen. Agriculture was adversely affected by the world-wide decline in primary produce and by fierce foreign competition in the British market. The overexpansion of world trade had caused such a fall in the demand for new ships that Belfast's shipyards were always working at less than half capacity and one had to close down in 1935. The decline in linen was permanent, brought about by the introduction of new fibres, high tariffs in the United States, the best customer, and the development of the industry overseas, where production costs were lower. The result was that Northern Ireland's rate of unemployment was significantly higher than that of Britain as a whole.

The alleviation of such economic problems was rendered more difficult by the fact that costs of production were higher in Northern Ireland than elsewhere in the United Kingdom because of the small scale of industrial production and the paucity of natural resources. Similarly, the modernisation of agriculture was hindered by the predominance of the small family farm and the almost legendary conservatism and fierce independence of Northern Ireland's farmers.

The other pressing problem facing Craig was the question of the legitimacy of the new regime in the eyes of the Catholic/nationalist minority. The parti-

tion of Ireland and the establishment of Northern
Ireland had been a victory for Unionists in the North,
which was never fully accepted by the minority who
hankered after a united Ireland. Not only had the
Catholic hierarchy and all shades of nationalist
opinion boycotted the new government at first, but
even when the constitutional Nationalists did enter
the Northern parliament in the mid-1920s, they did
so with reservations and refused to accept the role of
official Opposition. The minority's wholehearted
acceptance of Northern Ireland was essential both to
the realisation of Craig's wish for a united and contented North and to the elimination of a problem
that ultimately undermined the Stormont regime.

Yet essential though it was, the task of reconciliation was rendered particularly difficult by the sectarianism of the North and the irridentism of the
South. Such was the deep hostility and suspicion in
the North between nationalists and Unionists and
Catholics and Protestants that any concession to the
minority on such key issues as representation and
education could easily alienate Craig's Unionist supporters. Conversely, attempts to pander to the wishes
of his assured supporters on those issues would lay
him open to charges of gerrymandering and discrimination. Moreover, the attitude of Northern nationalists
to the Northern regime did not depend solely upon
the actions and attitude of the government there.
Southern claims to and actions against the North
often activated or reinforced the Northern minority's
hostility to partition by reminding them that they
were part of a larger nationalist community. After a
border agreement in 1925 most Nationalist MPs took
their seats in the Stormont parliament. But after the
formation of de Valera's first government in the
South in 1932, and his talk of Irish unity, they soon
withdrew and concentrated once again on the question of partition.

The solution of such pressing problems was made the more difficult by the nature of society in Northern Ireland. A small community, some 1¼ million people in an area the size of Yorkshire, where everybody knew everybody else's business, it was highly localised and politicised. Intense local and sectional interests often gave rise to a whole range of more or less representative pressure groups, from the Orange Order and the Protestant churches to local branches of the Ulster Farmers' Union, which demanded the ear, and sometimes the whole body and soul, of the administration.

What is more, they could be sure of getting at least the government's ear, for in such a small society it was almost impossible for ministers to be other than what Craig had promised in 1921 — 'at the disposal of the people'. On any and every issue ministers were likely to be buffeted by local opinion. Church-going ministers, as all had to be, were literally sitting targets for recurrent Orange and Protestant propaganda against the non-sectarianism of the 1923 Education Act. As Andrews explained to Craig during one such campaign,

> Already the Protestant pulpits are being used for defending what is called 'Protestant rights'. I had myself to listen to two lengthy harangues on the subject on Sunday last in Little's church at Castlereagh. The Orange order are working in co-operation with the churches, and I am afraid that the position will be difficult on the 12th July unless something is done.[1]

Ministers were also subjected to intense pressure on less momentous issues, for, as Pollock complained on one occasion, 'I cannot even discharge a redundant junior official without my life being made a burden.'[2] Whatever advantages such accessibility may have had,

the drawbacks were obvious. It hindered government
[94] initiative and the development of policies beneficial
to the region as a whole.

2

Craig never rose, or even seriously attempted to rise,
to the challenges thus posed. Rather, he seemed overwhelmed by them. He developed no long-term strate-
gies and seemed content to preside over the cabinet
and country rather than to lead. He liked to play
down difficulties and to see Northern Ireland as one
large happy family with himself as the benevolent and
popular pipe-smoking father-figure and head. In such
a paternalistic vein did he gently scold all those who
were in danger of bringing Northern Ireland into dis-
repute, like the farmers and milk retailers who were
at one time engaged in a particularly acrimonious dispute over milk prices. On 6 November 1931 he told a
conference of the combatants:

> In such a small area as ours it is a much happier
> position of affairs if we are able to arrange our dif-
> ferences ourselves, and the public are very much
> more satisfied when we are able to do so. . . .
> Outside our area of Ulster the daily reports in the
> bigger Press in London and so on are a very great
> hurt to us here. . . . I place more reliance upon a
> settlement tonight than I can tell you. . . . I make a
> strong appeal to both sides. . . . Lady Craigavon is
> anxious that we should go for tea and I think we
> will adjourn for that purpose.[3]

It was a style suited to Craig's personality — affable,
approachable, pragmatic, and with no pretence to
intellectual brilliance or political imagination. It was,
however, scarcely suited to the problems facing
Northern Ireland.

Craig's main responsibility as Prime Minister was to lead and to co-ordinate the activities of his cabinet, but he gave neither direction nor coherence. His general view was that having appointed ministers, he should allow them to get on with their jobs with the minimum of interference and should support them in face of criticism. No minister was ever forced to resign, with the result that Craig's cabinet became aged and decrepit. At the beginning of the 1930s it contained two octogenarians, and although both had disappeared by April 1937, Craig's remaining colleagues were hardly healthy and dynamic. According to Spender, since 1925 the permanent head of the Ministry of Finance and the Civil Service, the Minister of Home Affairs 'is much more ill than is generally known' and 'seems incapable of giving his responsible officials coherent directions on policy'. The Minister of Labour 'is so ill that everyone knows he will not return'. Then there was the Minister of Commerce, 'who is abroad at a time when his Department is being subjected to violent criticism & whose officials can never depend upon', and the Chief Whip 'whose Dr told me should retire for his own sake, but who does not wish to do so till certain ambitions are satisfied'.[4]

Such loyalty put Craig in a quandary when there was disagreement between ministers or departments. Yet Craig solved the dilemma by allowing matters to drift and hoping that ministers would themselves settle differences. Appealed to by the Ministry of Finance in July 1932 to resolve differences between Home Affairs and Labour, which were making nonsense of a government economy drive, Craig simply replied that Bates and Andrews, the respective ministers, 'were such personal friends that he felt assured that they would have no difficulty in adjusting any matters which might arise from this difference in procedure'.[5] In reality the contrary was true.

[96] This is not to suggest that Craig lacked initiative or authority. When he chose to exert himself the cabinet accepted his lead and toed the line, particularly on the only two issues guaranteed to galvanise him into action — partition and Northern Ireland's position as part of the United Kingdom. Here Craig served Northern Ireland, or at least Ulster Unionists, well. Partition remained; Northern Ireland's borders remained inviolate as the dreaded Boundary Commission came to nought; and after the early 1920s the existence of Northern Ireland as part of the United Kingdom was never seriously questioned.

Craig contributed much to such stability, particularly by the restraint he exercised in the years 1922—25 when the threat of the Boundary Commission hung over his country. Admittedly, disillusionment with the South, particularly after the events of 1922, internal political difficulties and increasing age and ill-health made Craig a more unbending upholder of partition. But he was equally determined not to provoke a confrontation with the South or to cause it any undue loss of face. Such concern led him to defy the Orange Order and finally dismiss by administrative order that partisan police officer, Nixon, after the latter had made a provocative speech pledging that the loyalists of Belfast would rush to the aid of their fellows on the border in the event of an invasion from the South. And in the discussions which led to the shelving of the Boundary Commission's report and to the tripartite agreement of 3 December 1925, by which the imperial, Free State and Northern Ireland governments formally confirmed the six-counties border, Craig won not only the gratitude of his own supporters but also the respect of Free State ministers.

Parliament presented him with a silver Celtic cup, the plinth of which was inscribed with the words

'NOT AN INCH', while the council of Aughnacloy, a small town lying on the Tyrone—Monaghan border-line, passed a resolution thanking Craig for settling 'the vexed and perplexing Boundary question, which has been hanging over the Border districts like a pall for the last four years, causing unrest and uneasiness to all the Loyalists in Northern Ireland'. On the other hand, his honesty and openness during the negotiations were much appreciated by Cosgrave, the Free State premier, who later recalled that

> Lord Craigavon improved on acquaintance. It is but just and fair to his memory to say that we found him honourable and straightforward. I never knew him to finesse, and he never sought to break a conference to his own advantage when he had the opportunity. He was in my opinion a loss to that greater Ireland which the statesmanship of his time had been unable to bring into being.[6]

It is true that Craig was not above exploiting the border question for his own political purposes, as in his response to the 1937 Éire constitution, which recognised the *de facto* position of Northern Ireland but claimed sovereignty over the whole island. His decision to hold a general election in February 1938 on the question arose less from fear that the border was in imminent danger than from the need to rally his supporters in order to squash growing Unionist criticism of his government's failure to solve pressing economic and social problems. The stratagem was successful, but its use was not entirely cynical, for Craig remained a deeply committed Unionist. Partition and Northern Ireland's position as part of the United Kingdom remained matters of passionate concern, which continued to exercise him in the very last months of his premiership, shortly before and during the early part of the Second World War. In

April 1939 and again in May 1940 he vainly pressed
the imperial government to extend to Northern Ireland the compulsory military service recently introduced in Britain. While he was anxious to underline
the North's loyalty and support for the war effort,
the imperial government was loath to offend the sus-
ceptibilities of nationalists in North and South. On
the other hand, in the summer of 1940 he so firmly
reiterated his government's determination to maintain the border that the imperial government was
forced to abandon its wishful thinking that an offer
of Irish unity might persuade Éire to abandon its
neutrality and place its ports at the disposal of the
Allies.

Such constitutional questions apart, the only issue
on which Craig took a consistent and informed
interest was the construction of the new parliament
buildings at Stormont. His longest and most passionate
letters to the cabinet secretariat related to the design
of concrete fencing posts on the Stormont estate!
Otherwise his handling of affairs was erratic and un-
predictable and formed no part of any overall strategy.

Thus he never at any time seriously grappled with
Northern Ireland's economic problems. Divine Pro-
vidence was assigned a key role in his economic philosophy, and despite his early flirtation with tariff reform, he basically believed in *laissez-faire.* He had
little confidence in man's ability to order the course
of economic development and seemed to take comfort in the notion that Northern Ireland's difficulties
were not unique but were the product of the disloca-
tion caused by the First World War and world-wide
depression. He was willing to support the various pro-
jects put forward by individual departments, particularly the Ministry of Finance's policy of guarantee-
ing loans to help the shipyards and the Ministry of
Agriculture's insistence upon compulsory marketing

schemes, but this was the extent of Craig's contribution to the reconstruction of agriculture and industry. He might support the policy of a particular ministry, but he could neither conceive of an overall economic strategy nor even co-ordinate the activities of the different departments involved in economic development.

The fate of the new-industries legislation of the 1930s is a case in point. The policy was ill-considered and poorly executed. The initial legislation was adopted not as the result of careful consideration. Rather, it was sprung on ministers and their departments in October 1931 by Craig during a campaign for elections to the imperial parliament. In order to rebut charges of government apathy in face of rising unemployment, Craig announced that rent-free sites would be offered to industrialists wishing to establish new industries. It was then left to the different departments to divine what Craig really had in mind and to hammer out the details; and the cabinet discussions of the consequent measure centred not around how far the provision of free sites would really attract new industries, but around how important it was that the government should avoid 'becoming owners of the land' and being 'left with sites which would become a charge on the Exchequer'.[7] As far as Craig was concerned, the important thing was to be seen to have a policy, regardless of whether or not it was effective.

He was likewise ineffectual in his handling of the one part of his job he really did enjoy — acting as a channel of communication between his and the imperial governments. On this ground he used to justify his prolonged sojourns at Cleeve Court, his house on the Thames, writing on 31 May 1926 to his acting Prime Minister, Pollock: 'I go to Town tomorrow for an important Dinner at which I shall

meet a mixture of the Leaders here, including your
[100] friend Philip Snowden: in this and other ways I keep
in touch with what is going on and if there is anything
of interest to relate I will let you know at once.'[8] In
1921–22 Craig had made full use of such contacts to
forward Northern Ireland's interests, but after then
he was less inclined to become involved in hard and
detailed bargaining, which he left to his ministers and,
more often than not, his officials. He preferred to
have, and placed great faith in, little generalised chats
with imperial ministers. Usually such optimism was
misplaced, a reflection of, as one senior Treasury
official put it, Craig's tendency 'to assume that
decisions are in his favour, unless it is made unusually
clear what the decisions are'.[9]

This affability was not without advantages. It helped
to damp down the tensions between regional and
central authorities inherent in any devolved system of
government but especially in that set up by the 1920
Government of Ireland Act. Different Northern Ireland and imperial perspectives often emerged on a
wide range of issues, but Craig prevented any disrup-
tion by fully adhering to the policy enunciated to
Churchill in 1922 during the dispute over the Local
Government Bill, namely, 'that no issue should arise
publicly upon which it could be urged by those with
whom he had to work in the North, that either he
had scored a personal success over HMG or, alterna-
tively, he had given way weakly to HMG'.[10]

The trouble was that Northern Ireland paid the
price for such harmony, since Craig was more responsive to the needs of the United Kingdom and Empire
rather than those of Northern Ireland, particularly on
such vital matters as trade and finance where his
government was so dependent on Westminster. After
the Colwyn Award had broken down at the end of
the 1920s and his government was forced to under-

take repeated and humiliating begging expeditions to the Treasury to avoid recurrent budget deficits, Craig made only half-hearted efforts to persuade Westminster to put Northern Ireland's finances on a permanently sound footing by an amendment of the financial provisions of the 1920 act. A very convincing case could be made out for amendment, but the imperial government refused to take such a controversial step, which, besides increasing its financial obligations to the North, would have had serious implications for its policy during its economic war with the South. The budget thus continued to be balanced by a series of 'fudges' and 'wangles' and 'dodges and devices' giving 'gifts and subventions within the ambit of the Government of Ireland Act so as to save the Northern Ireland Government from coming openly on the dole as Newfoundland did'.[11] This failure to secure an adequate and guaranteed income seriously stultified the work of government, both local and regional, with ultimately tragic consequences.

Similarly, Craig made little effort to ensure that Westminster, which retained powers over external trade, took adequate measures to protect Northern Ireland's flagging trade and industry. When in the 1920s the Board of Trade rejected an almost unanimous demand from Northern Ireland for a measure of protection for the ailing linen industry, Craig, despite constant badgering by Andrews, refused to make the rejection an issue between the two governments. This was partly because he feared that unsuccessful intervention on his part 'may draw down upon ourselves adverse criticism from those whom we are anxious to befriend', but largely because he was ever ready to condone British actions and to see, as he explained to Andrews on 29 July 1927, a 'deeper significance in the Government action than is allowed to appear on the surface. The cotton interests are very powerful and we can never fathom the extent [102] of their activities!'[12] Even when continued criticism of the rejection and the prospect of a general election in 1929 prompted Craig to promise action, he eventually allowed the matter to hang fire, for, after discussion with imperial ministers, he could not bring himself to embarrass the new Labour government, which was divided on the issue of free trade and protection.

It was the same story in the Anglo-Éire negotiations of 1938, which resulted in the handing back of the Treaty ports to Éire and the conclusion of financial and trade agreements favourable to the South. Despite the emphatic assertions of his official biographer, Craig did not protest vehemently against the handing back of the ports as likely to endanger the Empire in wartime. What concerned Northern Ireland and Craig in the negotiations was the prospect of a trade agreement which would allow goods from Éire almost free entry into the United Kingdom but still restrict United Kingdom exports to the South. So unfavourably did ministers regard the likely implications of the agreement for the North's economy that resignation and the holding of a general election were seriously considered by Sir Basil Brooke, then Minister of Agriculture, and Andrews, then Minister of Finance and, because of Craig's ill-health, charged with representing the North's views to the imperial government.

The prospect of such opposition alarmed imperial ministers, who regarded as essential the North's acceptance of the trade agreement. They feared that opposition would excite sympathy in Britain and, by stimulating criticism of the whole negotiations, hinder the United Kingdom's reconciliation with Éire and undermine the whole policy of international conciliation then so dear to certain ministers. Thus on 8 April

1938 Neville Chamberlain, then Prime Minister, urgently appealed to 'My dear James' to come to the rescue and not to hinder a settlement with Éire just at a time when

> in my anxieties over the international situation it has become almost essential for me to show some evidence that the policy of peace by negotiation can be successful. I have good hopes that I shall be able to bring forward an Anglo-Italian agreement as evidence of this, but if I can accompany that with an Anglo-Irish agreement it would greatly add to the impression made upon the world. And it is very necessary that an impression of solidarity here should be made, and not least in Berlin.[13]

Craig could not resist such a personal and portentous appeal. He took over the handling of Northern Ireland's case from Andrews, dispensed with the services of officials in his discussions with imperial ministers and officials, and quickly settled. Admittedly, he settled for a price — a bribe, as Treasury officials contemptuously called it; but the price, some ill-defined financial concessions, was a much lower one than his ministers and officials had advocated to compensate Northern Ireland for the economic and political difficulties thought likely to ensue from the Anglo-Éire trade agreement.

The root of the trouble was that Craig increasingly came to resemble the proverbial cushion which takes on the imprint of the last person who sat upon it. Too often his views on affairs of state, high or low, were determined by the attitude of the last person or deputation he had spoken to. Such responsiveness and accessibility were the hallmark of his annual tours of the country. First undertaken in 1922 to assuage the fears of Unionists under attack in the border areas, these tours soon became occasions for

Craig to listen to local grievances and problems and to [104] hand out largesse, particularly by, as he once put it, 'distributing bones' to local authorities.[14] Officials and sometimes colleagues railled against such disregard for established bureaucratic procedures, but by occasionally resulting in speedy decision-making it contributed no little to Craig's personal popularity. As one grateful newspaper commented during Craig's 1927 tour, shortly after he had been created Viscount Craigavon of Stormont,

> The visit of Lord Craigavon to Cookstown on Wednesday was memorable as the first visit of any Premier to our district in his official, as distinct from his party position. He came as the Premier, prepared to hear anything that the people had to say, and to judge on the spot. It is particularly gratifying to the ratepayers of the Rural and Urban districts to know that when his attention had been called to the injustice which existed in regard to the upkeep of the road from Orritor quarry to Cookstown railway station, which would have baffled the efforts of the Councils to have remedied through the ordinary channels, when it would have been strangled with red tape by permanent officials, his Lordship (with the assent of the Minister of Home Affairs, in whose department it was), swept the red tape aside in a regal fashion and uttered his fiat — let it be done from this very day. That, in itself, justified our expectations from his visit, and we are grateful alike for the manner of doing it as for the act itself.[15]

All areas, whether Protestant or Catholic, Unionist or nationalist, could profit from these tours. One of Craig's happiest trips was in 1930 to Galloon Island in Lough Erne. Its inhabitants, most of whom were nationalists, could reach the mainland only by their clumsy 'cots', in one of which Craig himself ventured. The experience prompted Craig to remedy the [105] islanders' plight by having a bridge built linking the island to the mainland.

This responsiveness stemmed partly from Craig's good nature and pragmatism but largely from his almost pathological fear of opposition within Northern Ireland. Despite his large and assured parliamentary majority, he displayed after 1922 an almost indecent degree of political timidity. It is true that his Protestant temperance critics may be excused for having thought otherwise, as they succumbed in the 1929 election to a swingeing counter-attack by the Prime Minister. But this was a special case, since the thinly disguised prohibitionist campaign, with its talk of '17,000 drunkards in Ulster' and '20,000 children deprived of food and affection in Belfast', could be represented as an attack on the state. 'It is rather a scandal', Craig retorted, 'for certain persons to paint the character of Ulstermen as black as they do. I have not banged the door on negotiations, but I am not going to be dragooned.'[16] Generally, however, while, and perhaps because, he accepted as virtually inevitable the hostility of the Catholic/nationalist minority, he was terrified of divisions among Unionists. Not merely did he believe it his duty to safeguard the position of Northern Ireland, but, like all politicians, he was anxious to remain in office.

Frequently fear of opposition led to inaction. In 1928 fear of upsetting farmers by increasing contributions caused Craig to delay for two more years Andrews's attempt to bring health insurance into line with the rest of the United Kingdom. The time to do so, he told Andrews on 13 June 1928, 'will be immediately *after* our General Election. The effects of any unpopularity will then have worn off before another appeal to the country at the end of four or

five years.'[17] Occasionally his apprehension led to
[106] positive action. Sometimes this was beneficial, particularly in respect of the support Craig generally
gave Andrews in maintaining the major cash social
services on a par with those in Britain. More often
than not, though, Craig's responses and whole style of
government only intensified the problems facing
Northern Ireland, particularly in relation to the structure of government and the minority question.

3

Since the unsatisfactory distribution of powers between the regional and local authorities was one of
biggest obstacles to prompt and efficient government
and thus to the modernisation of society and the
economy, rationalisation and a clearer definition of
responsibilities should have been obvious priorities.
Craig's colleagues recognised this, but his attitude
both precluded such far-reaching reforms and so
compounded existing complications and confusions
as to stunt initiative.

Exposure to the blandishments of a pressure group
could readily convince Craig that he had learned the
truth of the matter in hand and was in a position to
controvert expert opinion and upset an established
line of cabinet policy. Thus on his return from a visit
to Londonderry city during his 1927 tour Craig
quickly dismissed the serious reservations of ministers and officials about the wisdom of continuing
to subsidise an unprofitable light railway which served
the port of Londonderry and its Donegal hinterland.
He told the cabinet on 1 March 1927 that during his
recent tour 'he had gone into the matter very fully.
He had come to the conclusion that to allow this
Railway to close would be a disaster for Londonderry.'[18] Such intervention discouraged the exercise

of independent judgment on the part of ministers and officials, particularly the latter who later complained: 'We had been so often overruled by the Prime Minister's decisions that we did not feel justified in assuming a non possumus attitude.'[19]

Craig's policy of 'distributing bones' to local authorities largely arose out of his fear of their influence and the likely trouble such well-entrenched bodies could create for his infant government. As he warned the Junior Minister of Home Affairs on 5 June 1924 during a dispute over housing with Belfast Corporation, 'We always have to bear in mind that the City represents in many respects one-half of Northern Ireland and therefore requires careful handling.'[20] Such an accommodating approach simply reinforced the unhelpful position and attitudes of local authorities and hardly made for prompt, efficient or economical government. Local authorities were encouraged to postpone action in the hope of getting government money; spheres of responsibility were blurred; and resentment was created among those authorities not afforded similar treatment. Indeed, Craig's attitude so devalued relations between his government and local councils that one very competent but increasingly disenchanted official complained that 'The only way to get money from the Government is to make yourself unpleasant and then interview the Prime Minister.'[21]

Similarly, Craig's attitude helped to prevent the parliament of Northern Ireland from becoming either an effective debating chamber or an important element in the process of decision-making in the North. In many respects the new parliament's prospects were never very bright. Its powers were strictly limited; it attracted very few people of talent and energy; and it always had a large Unionist majority. But Craig never encouraged the elaborate parliament he had done so much to establish to overcome its limitations. On the [108] contrary, he did much to ensure that it became simply a rubber stamp. He sought to avoid criticism on some controversial issues by pleading that since they fell within the competence of the Westminster parliament, they should not even be discussed in the Northern parliament. Even on matters within its competence, Craig discouraged parliament from exercising initiative and independent judgment. As far as he was concerned, parliament should follow the government's lead and readily endorse proposals, especially those agreed between the government and such vested interests as local authorities. Thus in 1924 he virtually instructed a disgruntled House of Commons, then consisting only of Unionists, to accept new housing legislation, because, he said,

> I always feel that if we can get the Corporation to work hand in hand with us in a great ameliorative Measure like this we are doing infinite good to the people, whereas if there is a division of opinion, even on some financial matter of this kind, it shows that the two great bodies, the Parliament of Northern Ireland and the Corporation of Belfast, are not able to see eye to eye, which is a great mistake and, unfortunately, a great cause of unpleasantness amongst those who ought to be working harmoniously along the same lines. . . . After all they are a body that are up against serious problems. They have an intimate knowledge of the difficulties that arise in connection with the erection of working-class houses, and all that we can say as a Government is, 'How can we help them?'[22]

Not only did Craig's style complicate and devalue the ordinary processes of government in Northern Ireland, it also helped to deepen divisions in society. Craig showed such insensitivity and such lack of foresight and imagination in dealing with the minority question that he helped to confirm the minority's initial alienation from his regime.

Craig himself would have been surprised by such a verdict. Although, like most Ulster Presbyterians, he was hostile to the claims of the Catholic priesthood, he evinced no hostility towards individual Catholics, lay or clerical, and was punctilious in inviting the hierarchy to official functions, usually to no avail. Personally, too, he was on good terms with individual Nationalists and welcomed their participation in parliament. He had a genuine affection and respect for Joe Devlin, the leader of the Northern Nationalists, a liking which on one occasion led him to Celtic Park, the Gaelic football ground in Belfast, to watch greyhound racing. And his neighbourly habit of dropping in on ailing friends extended to his Nationalist neighbour, Paddy O'Neill, the MP for Mourne, during the latter's fatal illness.

Yet affability and personal humanity did not prevent Craig from hindering the task of reconciliation. Many of the minority's complaints against his regime were often exaggerated and misplaced. The regime was neither vindictive nor oppressive. Moreover, Craig's most unfortunate pronouncements upon the Protestant nature of his regime can largely be explained by his need to make a rhetorical response to events in the South. As he explained to one Nationalist critic, in the South they had boasted and 'still boast of Southern Ireland being a Catholic State. All I boast of is that we are a Protestant Parliament and a Protestant State.'[23] Nevertheless, Craig was tactless and did play a key role in promoting the discrimination which his government undoubtedly practised against the minority in certain vital matters. His avowed aim was always to maintain Northern Ireland as a bulwark against a united Ireland, but he tried to achieve this in

ways which ultimately led to the collapse of Stormont.
[110] Instead of making a sustained attempt to win over the
minority by assuaging their fears and suspicions, he
preferred to concentrate on maximising his party's
support and sustaining Unionist control in the North.
In fact Craig could never rise above his position as
leader of the Ulster Unionists. Narrow party considerations rather than broad considerations of state dictated
his attitude on such sensitive issues as government
employment, representation and education.

Few Catholics were employed in the Civil Service
or the police force. Although they comprised some 33
per cent of the population, they never came anywhere
near to achieving that proportion of government
posts. Throughout Craig's premiership their position
so deteriorated that by the time of his death they filled
only some 10 per cent of the lower ranks of the Civil
Service and less than 6 per cent of the higher grades.
They fared only marginally better in the RUC, where
in 1936 they formed some 17 per cent of the force.

It had certainly not been Craig's intention to have
an overwhelmingly Protestant government service,
and initially one-third of the RUC was intended to be
Catholic. Yet he did little to attract Catholic recruits
and much to deter potential applicants and discourage
serving officers. It was certainly not easy to be a
Catholic in the service of the government of Northern
Ireland, and Craig only increased these difficulties. He
tolerated the bigotry of his Minister of Home Affairs,
who refused to trust Catholics with any confidential
work, not even operating the Stormont telephone
exchange; and he alway treated seriously the numerous
complaints from Protestants and Unionists about the
alleged employment of vast numbers of so-called dis-
loyalists in the Civil Service and police at the expense
of loyalists. In 1924 his ordering of a prolonged inves-
tigation into the obviously outlandish allegations of

the Ulster Protestant Voters' Defence Association, a Belfast Orange group, prompted the Inspector-General of the RUC to protest against this 'effort to bring unfair influence to bear to the detriment of RC members of the Force', which militated 'against efficiency as it tends to undermine the confidence of the men in their superiors'.[24] The pattern did not alter with time. Ten years later Craig responded sympathetically to a 'vile persecution' by the Orange Order of a Catholic estate worker at Stormont, thus forcing the permanent head of the Civil Service, Spender, to complain bitterly to the Cabinet Secretary on 8 November 1934:

> If the Prime Minister is dissatisfied with our present system [of recruitment], I think the only course would be for the Government to come out in the open and to say that only Protestants are admitted to our Service. I should greatly regret such a course, and am quite convinced . . . that we are getting loyal service from all those who have entered our Service.[25]

Likewise, Craig never did all that he could have done to persuade the Catholic/nationalist minority to participate fully in parliament. He had learned nothing from the controversy in 1922 over the abolition of PR in local elections, and in 1929 took full and personal responsibility for its abolition in parliamentary elections, even though minorities in the North had made it clear that they regarded it as an invaluable safeguard, both actual and symbolic. In vain did Devlin, the Nationalist leader, ask the House of Commons:

> Is there any Government that would not have called the minority into council and have stated: 'We do not think Proportional Representation works very well, but you think it is a safeguard. Are you willing to retain it, or are you willing to consult with

us as to a substitute for it?' That is what a reasonable body of men would have done.[26]

In fact Craig never considered consulting the
minority. He had never liked PR, which he regarded
as utterly useless as a minority safeguard. He never
bothered to explain why he thought that, and there is
no evidence to suggest that he ever thought about the
possible adverse consequences of the abolition of PR
for the nature of government and politics. Its advo-
cates maintained that the chief merit of PR was that
it encouraged and facilitated the widest representation of political opinion in parliament, but to Craig
this was its greatest disadvantage. He was not interested
in securing a varied parliament but in maintaining
partition and the status of Northern Ireland. He disliked a system which allowed the return of Independents and Labour members who placed as much
emphasis on bread-and-butter issues as on the border
question, and who might, therefore, mislead electors
into voting for a united Ireland. Thus the abolition of
PR in parliamentary elections was designed to clarify
the issue between Unionism and nationalism and, as
Craig put it, to get into parliament 'men who are for
the Union on the one hand or who are against it and
want to go into a Dublin Parliament on the other'.[27]
Craig's desire to make public bodies safe for
Unionism was shared by all other Unionists, but
Craig was more subtle. If his supporters had had
their way, there would have been virtually no Catholic,
nationalist, independent or Labour representation in
parliament or on local councils. As Prime Minister,
Craig had to be more circumspect, to avoid giving the
outside world the impression that he was actively discriminating against minorities. Yet although less
blatant than his supporters, he still sympathised with
their general aims and so altered electoral boundaries,

parliamentary and local, as to give substance to charges of gerrymandering. As he told Londonderry Unionists who in 1936 wanted to shore up their dwindling majority on the city council, 'You may rest assured that all of us have the one aim in view, and that is to maintain the integrity of the Maiden City.'[28]

It was Craig too who was largely responsible for subsequent amendments to the 1923 Education Act, the Londonderry act, so as to make state schools safe for Protestantism. The Londonderry act had sought to transform education in the North by establishing a non-sectarian system combining efficiency with popular local control. Designed to obliterate the clerical control and poverty which had characterised the National system under the Union, the act was in broad harmony with the ideas preached by Craig during his time as a backbencher in the imperial parliament. Yet changes in 1925 and 1930 produced a system effectively endowing Protestantism and discriminating against Catholics, particularly by providing for compulsory simple Bible instruction. Protestants could without violating their consciences allow their schools to be run by local authorities and thus maintained wholly out of public funds, but the same option was not open to conscientious Catholics. Such differential treatment, which probably contravened the 1920 act, was roundly condemned by Daniel Mageean, the Catholic Bishop of Down and Connor, as

> against all principles of justice and equity. . . . We form a large portion of the population, and have more children attending primary elementary schools than any other religious denomination. We ask for no privilege, but we claim equality of treatment with our fellow citizens, and we demand our rights.[29]

Craig never understood the nature of Catholic

objections to the 1930 Education Act, because he [114] never understood the nature of Catholicism. He could not grasp that simple Bible teaching, even from a version of the Bible acceptable to them, was anathema to Catholics and thus a barrier to the transfer of their schools to public control. However, even had he understood Catholic teaching better, it is unlikely that his attitude to the amendment of the Londonderry act would have been any different. It was powerful pressure engineered at crucial political times by the Protestant churches and the Orange Order, rather than educational principles or wider considerations of state, that led Craig to override the views of both the Ministry of Education and local education authorities and compromise the non-sectarianism of the original act, so dear to the heart of Londonderry, the first Minister of Education.

In March 1925, when Londonderry was away in England, Craig met Protestant and Orange leaders and agreed to amend the 1923 act in order to preserve party unity on the eve of a crucial general election on the border. In the following June he successfully persuaded Londonderry to make further concessions and thus avoid the hostile resolutions which were being prepared for the forthcoming Orange Day demonstrations. Londonderry's successor as Minister of Education, Viscount Charlemont, learned the lesson, and when agitation began to gather momentum again he reported to Craig on 5 July 1928 that he had not 'banged and bolted the door against possible amendment in the future, so that if you and the Cabinet *do* feel that anything of the kind is advisable, the Government will not be exhibiting a *complete* volte-face!' [30] This was a realistic attitude, for Craig soon capitulated when the clergy and Orangemen threatened to campaign against the government in the 1929 general election on the slogan 'Protestantism in danger'. On

5 April 1929 Craig told the Northern Ireland Association of Education Committees, which vehemently
opposed further changes, that nothing should be done
'for political expediency which they thought was
wrong and against the best interests of the education
of their children' and that 'The more one heard, the
better the existing Act appeared to be working and
the more one was convinced that the difficulties were
not so much advanced by sincere educationists as by
carping critics.'[31] These were statesmanlike sentiments, but within a month, with a general election
looming large, Craig had decided that it would be
politically safer to undertake the further amendment
of the Londonderry act in line with all the clerical—
Orange demands.

Craig's handling of the education question was at
one with his handling of other sensitive issues. He
simply responded to immediate political needs and
was apparently incapable of judging the broad and
long-term effects of his actions. He was so responsive
to the claims of his supporters that he, and thus his
government also, was unable to correct the imbalance
created in the political system by the minority's
opting out and did much to accentuate that imbalance.
He may have done his best to moderate the more
extreme demands of his supporters, and he was always
concerned to present a plausible explanation of any
changes in electoral or education laws, but in the last
analysis Craig consistently used the power of the state
to further the interests of Protestantism and Unionism.

4

Craig's performance during his 'peacetime' premiership
provided a sad contrast to the courage and determination he had shown in erecting and defending his government in the stormy early months of its existence. The

limited achievements of the subsequent years provided an equally sad contrast to the promises he had made in 1921 of just, reformist and efficient government. No serious or sustained attempt was made to overcome the admittedly daunting difficulties facing Northern Ireland. The result was that the country became saddled with a ramshackle system of government, and a whole range of services, such as health, housing and education, remained underdeveloped in comparison with the rest of the United Kingdom. The economy continued to decay. And the divisions between Catholics and Protestants became more pronounced and institutionalised. It is true that the solution of such problems would have been beyond the ken of any leader, but what was particularly distressing in Craig's case was his failure to realise just how little was being achieved in the 1920s and 1930s and how many of his actions accentuated Northern Ireland's problems. It was enough for him that he remained in office and that Northern Ireland and the border continued to exist.

There had been signs in 1922, particularly in his handling of questions relating to law and order, of Craig's limitations as head of government in such a troubled and divided community. But what was surprising in subsequent years, and what requires explanation, is his almost total failure to assert and exert himself and the ease with which he constantly gave way in face of agitation and opposition.

One explanation for this collapse of judgment and initiative derives from the plight in which he and his government found themselves in the inter-war years. Wide formal responsibilities but little real power meant that they were confronted by large and intractable problems but had little room for manoeuvre. So enormous were the country's economic problems, and so little could his government do to alleviate them, that Craig was forced to take advantage of what few real powers he had to assert his authority and reward and retain the loyalty of his supporters. It was just unfortunate that these real powers related to the most sensitive issues dividing Northern Irish society. Craig may not, for example, have been able to solve the city of Londonderry's economic problems, which were caused by a general decline of the linen shirt industry and the South's economic policies, and which were, the Lord Mayor once reported, 'making loyalists feel "What is the use of staying under a Government that either don't care a d——n for our interests, or at any rate can't protect them."'[32] But he could at least ensure that his supporters remained in control of the city.

Yet, although large problems and limited powers reduced the range of policy options open to Craig, they do not explain why he failed to take full advantage of the limited options open to him, or why he took particular options, or why he refused to face up to problems, or why he so readily gave way to opposition rather than risk confrontation. The answer to such questions is that ill-health seriously undermined his capacity to work, let alone head a government.

It was his misfortune that he never fully recovered from a disease, akin to spotted fever, which had befallen him in the spring of 1915. The illness had kept him in bed for months, and he probably would have died but for the unremitting care of a certain Ulster bacteriologist. Craig, who had previously enjoyed good physical health and strength and had seldom been sick, had thereafter always to contend with disease. His hectic life in 1921—22 could have done little to help, so that during his premiership he was frequently incapacitated by illness, particularly in the winter months, when he was especially prone to bouts of influenza. Occasionally, too, his health

was further complicated by the recurrence of the ear
wound he had received during the South African War,
the pain from which was sometimes almost unbearable.

His health provided both a reason and an excuse to
escape from Northern Ireland for increasingly long
holidays. The first escape was to the south of France
in the winter of 1922—23, and the absences became
increasingly protracted as he undertook longer and
longer sea cruises. So marked was his penchant for
the sea that it was eventually said that only people
capable of undertaking long sea voyages need apply
for the premiership of Northern Ireland. Conscious
of criticism, Craig liked to justify his sojourns abroad
by arguing that he was acting as his country's com-
mercial salesman. And there was a grain of truth in
this. The promotion of Northern Ireland's trading
interests usually formed part of his programme. During a trip to Australasia, which took him away for
six months between September 1929 and March
1930, he did try to promote Northern Ireland's
trade. In Melbourne, where a display of Irish linen
had been arranged in honour of his arrival, he visited
every shop in the city where such goods were sold,
interviewing buyers and directors, and urging them to
buy linen from Northern Ireland in preference to any
other country.

These trips were not, however, undertaken for
Northern Ireland's benefit, but for Craig's. He revelled
in the sea and the atmosphere on board ship, especially
the deference accorded to him as a Prime Minister.
During a three-day journey between Australia and
New Zealand his wife recorded in her diary that he
'spent a good deal of his time on the bridge with
the Captain, being very fascinated by the gyro steer-
ing apparatus and a gadget for regulating the disposi-
tion of the cargo'. And when they disembarked at
Southampton on their return their fellow-passengers

gave them 'a very hearty send off, cheering lustily and singing "For They Are Jolly Good Fellows"!' So much importance did Craig attach to such cruises that not even his wife's health would deter him. When on 26 December 1935 the Craigs left Belfast to go to South America for three months his wife noted in her diary:

> I never felt less like travelling, still having a temperature, and would have given worlds not to go, but I knew it was James's only chance of getting the sea air which does him so much good, and he felt that if I could only just struggle on board, the change would probably put me right. However, I got a relapse subsequently, and was in bed the whole voyage, with a ship's doctor standing at my bedside saying, 'You know, Lady Craigavon, your pulse really appals me!'[33]

The extent to which failing powers and a desire to flee to sea deprived his government of leadership and direction was all too evident in his mishandling of what was to have been a determined effort on the part of his government in 1933—34 to secure its financial future once and for all by an amendment of the 1920 act. Craig was loath to become embroiled in such a complex and contentious issue by exploiting his political contacts in Britain, and when he was eventually persuaded to intervene he managed to make the very worst out of the very good case that could be made for amendment.

In the first instance, he almost jeopardised the goodwill that had gradually grown up between his Ministry of Finance and the imperial Treasury by at first agreeing and then refusing to implement certain financial reforms suggested by the latter. Indeed, Craig was so irritated by the Treasury's cautious and questioning response to his government's financial plight that he complained that there was 'a complete [120] misunderstanding among officials on the other side of the true position' in thinking that 'our accounts were as much subject to the scrutiny of the Treasury as those of the Admiralty or any other Department in London. This was quite wrong. Ulster was a Province and had its own elected Government.'[34] Yet, indignant though he was, he refused to devote time and attention to ironing out such misunderstandings. He did have an interview with his Conservative friends, Stanley Baldwin and Neville Chamberlain, then respectively deputy Prime Minister and Chancellor of the Exchequer, but he presented the Northern Ireland case so badly that the British ministers thought that he was willing to do the very opposite from what he had intended. They thought that Craig would no longer press for a revision of the 1920 act, but that Northern Ireland would continue to muddle through and meet any deficit by extra taxation or economies. This fundamental misunderstanding emerged only incidentally in the course of a telephone conversation between officials on another matter. But as Craig had already departed on a six-week cruise of the West Indies, the matter was settled to Northern Ireland's disadvantage, not by further high-level ministerial meetings but by correspondence between the Ministry of Finance and the Treasury.

Even when in Northern Ireland and not on the high seas, Craig found it increasingly difficult to give affairs, even the most congenial, his full attention for any length of time. The burdens of ill-health were increased by the distress occasioned by the death of old friends. He was particularly affected by the passing of his Minister of Finance, Pollock, in April 1937. So sorely grieved was he that although he went to the cemetery he could not remain for the burial. Indeed, 1937 was a particularly trying year for Craig. In the summer his blood pressure was very high and he was in danger of a stroke. He was so ill and tired that when King George VI and his Queen visited Northern Ireland on 28 July Craig had to abandon most of his duties to his wife. By the middle of August he was sufficiently well to move to a furnished house at Donaghadee, where he hoped the Co. Down air would make him strong again, but at the end of three weeks he had an attack of diverticulitis, a painful complaint akin to appendicitis, and was taken back to Stormont on doctor's orders. Before he had recovered from its effects the family scourge, influenza, struck him down again.

Such ill-health combined with advancing years to accentuate all the defects inherent in Craig's style of leadership. By 1938 the sixty-seven-year-old Craig was, according to his former admirer, Spender, 'so unwell that he cannot do more than an hour's concentrated work' and 'prefers to make quick hasty decisions rather than go fully into a question with his colleagues'. There was 'an entire absence of clear thinking and co-ordination', and

> Cabinet meetings seldom take place now, and the most important decisions are announced without any indication that they are the result of mature consideration, and very often the Ministers most concerned seem to be unaware of what is happening until an announcement is made in the Press.[35]

Indeed, Spender thought that Craig should be persuaded to resign, but Craig never seriously considered resignation. In truth, he had become increasingly reliant on his prime ministerial salary, for his long political career had eaten into his private fortune, which had diminished from £100,000 to £27,000. The perks of office were also dear to him, and even more to his wife. They were both delighted when in

January 1927 Craig was created Viscount Craigavon,
[122] and there was always the prospect of an earldom,
while Lady Craigavon liked to treat the cabinet
secretariat as her own private office and found the
highly paid Cabinet Secretary particularly useful for
telephoning Fortnum & Mason's in London to order
marmalade. Moreover, there was no real pressure for
his resignation. There was no obvious alternative
leader, and critics could always be vanquished by an
election on the border issue, as happened in February
1938. Although not well enough to campaign personally, Craig reaffirmed the Unionism of the North
and routed his Progressive Unionist critics in a general
election ostensibly called as a riposte to the new Éire
constitution with its claims to the North.

It was his fifth successive election victory, and he
thoroughly enjoyed being told by the *Daily Express*
that he was 'the one politician who can win an Election without even leaving his fireside'.[36] In these
circumstances he would find utterly perplexing the
notion that his premiership had been anything other
than a resounding success. But this very perplexity
would simply underline the extent of his failure to
realise, let alone resolve, the problems that had
faced his government and country.

Conclusion

Sunday 24 November 1940 was a quiet day in the Craig household. Craig, then almost seventy, had been taken ill the previous Thursday with a pain under his arm and a high temperature, but now seemed to be recovering. He read and dozed and chatted. At six o'clock he and his wife listened to the news on the radio. Then Lady Craigavon, after giving him his pipe and a detective story, went out to attend to their dearly loved grandson, sick with influenza. 'Are you all right?' she inquired at the door.[1] Craig nodded his head. When she returned an hour later he was dead.

The grief in Northern Ireland at his death was widespread and undisguised. And understandably so. For over thirty years he had dominated political life there. In so far as any one man was responsible for the partition of Ireland, it was Craig. He did not create the Ulster Unionist movement nor the conditions which had given rise to it, but he did give Ulster Unionists at a critical time a direction and coherence that made it impossible for any government at Westminster to force Home Rule on a united Ireland. When, too, it was decided to partition Ireland and establish not one but two Irish parliaments, it was Craig who got a six-counties Northern Ireland off the ground. By the same token, however, if any one man can be held responsible for the ultimate failure of Northern Ireland, it was Craig, for it was under his premiership that a pattern of government and politics emerged that ultimately led to the suspension in 1972 [124] of the Northern Ireland parliament.

Craig was the only man in Northern Ireland remotely capable of giving unity and direction to the new region. In 1921–22 there were signs that he would exert himself to ensure the establishment of a system of government and politics which combined enterprise with justice, honesty and impartiality. He defended his new government against pressure from both Britain and the South of Ireland, and at the same time he tried to moderate the often violent feelings of his supporters in the North. Under his leadership Northern Ireland survived the threat of anarchy in 1921–22 and emerged with a workable system of government and administration. Yet that effort seems to have exhausted Craig. Never again did he assert himself with such effect. It was true that he was tired and ill, but it was also true that he lacked the qualities to lead a government successfully. He was an effective organiser and administrator, and he could take resolute action, but he was able to organise and act only when there was a clearly defined and limited aim in view. What he lacked was charisma and the capacity to develop policies and direct their implementation. For much of his premiership he was content to let Northern Ireland drift with no overall sense of direction and to let the minority question fester. Perhaps he always needed a Carson to leaven his basic mediocrity.

Craig was ultimately a failure because he failed to do his utmost to ensure the stability and continued existence of the government and parliament he had done so much to create. Yet the failures of Northern Ireland were not the failures of leadership alone, for it is doubtful whether greater determination on his part would have fundamentally altered the course of events and secured the ultimate survival of Stormont. There were too many obstacles to the development of a healthy political life in Northern Ireland — natural economic disadvantages; a political culture characterised by sectarianism and localism; an unsatisfactory distribution of administrative and financial powers; and an irridentist Southern neighbour. In these circumstances only a very extraordinary Prime Minister could have even attempted to revitalise the economy or resisted the temptation to use in the interests of his supporters what powers of discrimination he possessed in respect of education, representation and justice.

Despite an extraordinary career, James Craig remained a very ordinary man, mastered by and not master of circumstances and events.

Bibliographical Note

Hitherto biographers of Craig have been handicapped by the dearth of both documentary evidence, since Craig left few personal papers, and scholarly secondary works essential to a proper understanding of a man whose career can be understood only in the context of Ulster Unionism and the operations of the government of Northern Ireland. Thus Hugh Shearman's *Not an Inch: A Study of Northern Ireland and Lord Craigavon,* London 1943, is well-written but slight. The official biography by St John Ervine, *Craigavon, Ulsterman,* London 1949, contains some useful information drawn from the proceedings of the Westminster and Northern Ireland parliaments, as well as Craig's South African War Diary and his wife's Diary (Public Record Office of Northern Ireland, D1415) and posthumous tributes to Craig, but it is unwieldy, uncritical and uninformative on Craig's premiership. However, the progressive availability of official and other papers in the Public Record Offices in Belfast and London, and the recent publication of a number of scholarly studies of Ulster Unionism and Northern Ireland, make possible a more comprehensive and critical account of Craig's career, particularly after 1920.

The most relevant of the official and semi-official papers desposited in the Public Record Office of Northern Ireland include minutes, correspondence and a working diary kept by Wilfrid Spender, the permanent head of the Ministry of Finance. The Cabinet Conclusions for Craig's premiership, 1921–40 (CAB 4/1–456) and his correspondence with the Cabinet Secretary, 1921–30 (PM 9/1–26) provide a convenient statement of Craig's views on various issues; while Spender's Financial Diary, 1931–44 (D715) constitutes an increasingly critical commentary on Craig's leadership. Particular issues may be followed up in individual cabinet or departmental files, such as: the state of Northern Ireland's finances (CAB 9A/3/1–5); the position of Catholics in government service (CAB 9A/90/1,2); law and order (CAB 6/27–31; 9B/4,18,201; 9G/19/1–3); the abolition of PR and the redrawing of electoral areas (CAB 9B/13/1–3; 9B/38/1; HA 14/161); tours of the border (CAB 9B/136); the amendment of the 1923 Education Act (CAB 9D/1/3–6,8,9); and the 1938 Anglo-Éire negotiations (CAB 9R/60/1–5).

The records of the imperial government deposited in the Public Record Office in London are particularly helpful on Northern Ireland's relations with the imperial and Southern Irish governments. Thus Craig's role in the shaping of the 1920 act and his defence of Northern Ireland's interests in 1921–22 are well documented in both cabinet and departmental files. The former include not only the Cabinet Conclusions, 1919–Aug. 1922 (CAB 23/18–30), but also the proceedings of the cabinet's various committees on Ireland (CAB 27/68–70,130,151,153–4, 156; 43/1–7). The relevant departmental records include the correspondence of the Colonial Office with the two Irish governments in 1922–23 (CO 739/1,14–19); the papers relating to the dispute over the abolition of PR in local elections in 1922 (HO 45/13371/463565); and the Treasury's reaction to Craig's financial demands (T 160/150/5814; 163/6/ G256/049). Again, Craig's decisive role in the 1938

Anglo-Éire negotiations is evident in the records of
[128] both the cabinet (CAB 27/524,527) and the Treasury
(T 160/747/14026/04).

Secondary works on Ulster Unionism before
1921 include general accounts by P. Buckland, *Irish
Unionism 2: Ulster Unionism and the Origins of
Northern Ireland, 1886–1922,* Dublin/New York
1973, and A. T. Q. Stewart, *The Ulster Crisis,* London
1967. In addition, P. J. Gibbon's *The Origins of
Ulster Unionism: The Formation of Popular Protestant Politics and Ideology in Nineteenth-Century
Ireland,* Manchester 1975, is a provocative Marxist
exploration of the socio-economic basis of the
movement. D. W. Miller's *Queen's Rebels: Ulster
Loyalism in Historical Perspective,* Dublin/New York
1978, shows how contractual theories of government
enabled Ulster Unionists to offer only conditional
loyalty to Westminster. F. Wright's 'Protestant
Ideology and Politics in Ulster', *European Journal
of Sociology* XIV (1973), 213–80, examines the
independent role of religious ideology in Northern
Ireland politics.

There is no adequate general history of Northern
Ireland since 1921, but F. S. L. Lyons's *Ireland since
the Famine,* rev. ed., London 1973, provides an introduction. Although it concentrates on the period since
1945, K. S. Isles and N. Cuthbert, *An Economic
Survey of Northern Ireland,* Belfast 1957, remains
the only substantial discussion of Northern Ireland's
economic and industrial problems and policies in the
inter-war years. The title of N. Akenson's *Education
and Enmity: The Control of Schooling in Northern
Ireland, 1920–1950,* Newton Abbot/New York 1973,
is self-explanatory. Finally, there are several studies
of devolution in the inter-war years. N. Mansergh's
*The Government of Northern Ireland: A Study of
Devolution,* London 1936, is largely a description of

the institutions of government, but R. J. Lawrence's *The Government of Northern Ireland: Public Finance and Public Services, 1921–1964,* Oxford 1965, provides an introduction to the complexities of Northern Ireland's finances and a useful summary of the achievements or otherwise of the region's experience of devolution in the inter-war years. While Mansergh and Lawrence were limited to published sources, P. Buckland's *The Factory of Grievances: Devolved Government in Northern Ireland, 1921 – 39,* Dublin/New York 1979, uses the government archives to analyse the process of decision-making and to present an indictment of the operation of devolved government in Northern Ireland.

[129]

References

PD   *Parliamentary Debates (Northern Ireland House of Commons)*
PRO   Public Record Office, London
PRONI   Public Record Office, Northern Ireland

Introduction (pp. 1–2)
1. St John Ervine, *Craigavon, Ulsterman*, London 1949, 4.

Chapter 1: Backbencher (pp. 3–14)
1. Ervine, 533.   2. *Ibid.*, 24.   3. *Ibid.*, 31.
4. *Ibid.*, 48.   5. *Ibid.*, 44.   6. *Ibid.*, 49.
7. *Ibid.*   8. *Ibid.*, 65.
9. P. Buckland, *Irish Unionism* 2: *Ulster Unionism and the Origins of Northern Ireland, 1886–1922*, Dublin/New York 1973, 42.
10. Ervine, 156.   11. *Ibid.*, 171–2.   12. *Ibid.*, 170.

Chapter 2: Rebel (pp. 15–49)
1. F. Wright, 'Protestant Ideology and Politics in Ulster', *European Journal of Sociology* XIV (1973), 224.
2. T. M. Johnstone, *Ulstermen: Their Fight for Fortune, Faith and Freedom*, Belfast 1914, 88, quoted by D. W. Miller, *Queen's Rebels: Ulster Loyalism in Historical Perspective*, Dublin/New York 1978, 117.
3. E. Saunderson, *Two Irelands: or, Loyalty versus Treason*, London 1884, 3, quoted *ibid.*, 110.
4. *PD*, xvi, 1091 (24 Apr. 1934).
5. *The Lessons of Craigavon*, Belfast 1911, quoted by Ervine, 193–5.
6. J. S. Sandars, private secretary, to A. J. Balfour, leader of the Conservative and Unionist Party, 20 Sep. 1908, British Museum, Add. MS.49765, ff. 175–8.
7. Ervine, 185.   8. *Ibid.*, 191.   9. *Ibid.*, 185.
10. *Ibid.*, 183.   11. Buckland, 48.   12. Ervine, 205.

13. *Ibid.*, 220.   14. *Ibid.*, 227.   15. *Ibid.*, 222.

16. A. T. Q. Stewart, *The Ulster Crisis*, London 1967, 63.

17. *Ibid.*, 64—5.   18. *Ibid.*, 193.   19. Ervine, 240.

20. *Ibid.*, 218—19.   21. *Ibid.*, 219.   22. *Ibid.*, 240.

23. *Ibid.*, 239.   24. PRONI, D1415/E/21.

25. Buckland, 100.   26. Ervine, 356.   27. *Ibid.*, 362.

28. *Ibid.*, 366, 368, 369.

29. C. Younger, *A State of Disunion*, London 1972, 186.

30. *Hansard*, 5th series, cxxvii, 989—90 (29 Mar. 1920).

31. Ervine, 369.

32. *Hansard*, 5th series, cxxxvi, 783 (16 Dec. 1920).

33. D. G. Boyce, *Englishmen and Irish Troubles: British Public Opinion and the Making of Irish Policy, 1918—22*, London 1972, 109—10.

34. *Hansard*, 5th series, cxxvii, 991 (29 Mar. 1920).

35. Younger, 189.

36. *Ulster and Home Rule: No Partition of Ulster*, Monaghan 1920, PRONI, D627/435.

37. *Ibid.*   38. Ervine, 365.   39. Buckland, 121.

40. T. Jones, *Whitehall Diary*, Vol. III: *Ireland, 1918—1925*, ed. K. Middlemas, London 1971, 28.

41. *Ibid.*, 38.   42. Ervine, 372.

Chapter 3: Statemaker (pp. 50—88)

1. Lady Craig's Diary, 8 Feb. 1921, PRONI, D1415/B/38.

2. Ervine, 373.

3. *PD*, i, 36—7 (23 Jun. 1921).

4. Londonderry to St Loe Strachey, 3 Jan. 1923, House of Lords Record Office, S/9/15/9.

5. Minute, 5 Oct. 1921, PRONI, CAB 6/27.

6. Ervine, 380, 418.   7. PRONI, PM 1/1.

8. *Ibid.*, PM 1/5.   9. Lady Craig's Diary, 13 May 1921.

10. Younger, 191—2.   11. Lady Craig's Diary, 5 May 1921.

12. Cabinet Conclusions, 26 Jan. 1922, PRONI, CAB 4/30/9.

13. F. S. L. Lyons, *Ireland since the Famine*, Fontana ed., London 1973, 427, 492.

14. Buckland, 130—1.

15. Lady Craig's Diary, 22 Jun. 1921.

16. Jones, 129.   17. Buckland, 148.

18. Lady Spender's Diary, 13 Feb. 1922, PRONI, D1633/2/26.

19. Lady Craig's Diary, 17 Dec. 1921, 4 Apr. 1922.

20. PRONI, CAB 6/27.   21. *Ibid.*

22. Craig to C. H. Blackmore, Assistant Cabinet Secretary, 5 Jun. 1922, and to Spender, 9 Jun. 1922, *ibid.*, PM 9/2.

[132] 23. L. Curtis, Colonial Office Adviser on Irish Affairs, to Churchill, 1 Sep. 1922, PRO, HO 45/13371/463565/1.

24. Lady Spender's Diary, 29 Jan. 1922.

25. Lady Craig's Diary, 5, 7 Nov. 1921.

26. Ervine, 461–2.

27. Notes on Belleek and Pettigo by S. G. Tallents, imperial representative in Northern Ireland, 13 Nov. 1922, PRO, CO 739/1.

28. R. Taylor, *Michael Collins*, New English Library ed., London 1970, 138.

29. Imperial Cabinet Conclusions, 30 May 1922, PRO, CAB 23/30.

30. *Ibid.*, T 163/6/G256/049.

31. O. Niemeyer to S. Baldwin, then Chancellor, 20 Nov. 1922, *ibid.*, T 160/150/5814/1.

32. *PD*, ii, 230 (28 Mar. 1922).

33. Cabinet Conclusions, 26 Jan. 1922, PRONI, CAB 4/30/9.

34. Lady Spender's Diary, 5 Feb. 1922.

35. Memo, 10 Feb. 1922, Birmingham University Library, AC/5/2/3.

36. Lady Spender's Diary, 6 Apr. 1922.

37. Pact reproduced in D. Macardle, *The Irish Republic*, Corgi ed., London 1968, 894–6.

38. *PD*, ii, 598 (23 May 1922).

39. Lady Craig's Diary, 21 Jan. 1922.

40. Craig to St Loe Strachey, 14 Apr. 1922, House of Lords Record Office, S/4/15/6.

41. PRO, CO 739/14.

42. *Ibid.*, HO 45/13371/463565/1.

43. Craig to Spender, 18 Jul. 1922, PRONI, PM 9/4.

44. Craig to Spender, 3 May 1922, *ibid.*, PM 9/2.

45. *Ibid.*, PM 9/1.

46. Curtis to Churchill, 1 Sep. 1922, PRO, HO 45/13371/463565/1.

47. *PD*, i, 443 (7 Dec. 1921).

48. 3 May 1922, PRONI, PM 9/2.

49. Spender to Craig, 22 Apr. 1922, *ibid.*, PM 9/1.

50. *Ibid.*, CAB 9B/18.

51. Craig to Blackmore, 29 Aug. 1922, *ibid.*, PM 9/4.

52. Memo, 6 Sep. 1922, PRO, CO 739/1.

53. PRONI, PM 9/3.

54. Solly Flood to Watt, 28 Sep. 1922, *ibid.*, CAB 6/30.

55. *Ibid.*, PM 9/2.

56. *PD*, ii, 1149 (7 Dec. 1922).

Chapter 4: Failure (pp. 89—122)

1. 17 Jun. 1925, PRONI, CAB 9D/1/5.

2. *PD*, xi, 486 (12 Jun. 1929).

3. PRONI, CAB 9E/111/1.

4. W. Spender, Financial Diary, Mar.—Oct. 1938, manuscript note between pp. 122—3, *ibid.*, D715.

5. *Ibid.*, 1932—33, p. 25.   6. Ervine, 507—8.

7. Cabinet Conclusions, 18 Nov. 1931, PRONI, CAB 4/293/39.

8. *Ibid.*, PM 9/16.

9. Sir Richard Hopkins, Second Secretary, to N. Chamberlain, then Chancellor, 16 May 1933, PRO, T 160/550/6562/021/1.

10. *Ibid.*, HO 45/13371/463565/1.

11. Hopkins to N. Chamberlain, 16 May 1933, *ibid.*, T 160/550/6562/021/1; Hopkins to Sir Frank Phillips, an Under-Secretary at the Treasury, 8 Feb. 1938, *ibid.*, T 160/1138/15586/1.

12. PRONI, PM 9/18.

13. *Ibid.*, CAB 9R/60/3.

14. Financial Diary, 1932—33, p. 1.

15. *Mid-Ulster Mail*, 19 Feb. 1927.

16. J. F. Harbinson, *The Ulster Unionist Party, 1882—1973: Its Development and Organisation*, Belfast 1973, 218.

17. PRONI, CAB 9C/15.

18. *Ibid.*, CAB 4/187/36.

19. Financial Diary, 1 Jan.—30 Nov. 1934, p. 237.

20. PRONI, CAB 9B/45/1.

21. Spender to Blackmore, 30 Dec. 1927, *ibid.*, CAB 9B/136.

22. *PD*, iv, 1521 (23 Oct. 1924).

23. *Ibid.*, xvi, 1095 (24 Apr. 1934).

24. Lt-Col. C. G. Wickham to Watt, 6 Mar. 1924, PRONI, CAB 9A/90/1.

25. *Ibid.*

26. *PD*, x, 1533 (27 Mar. 1929).

27. *Ibid.*, viii, 2276 (25 Oct. 1927).

28. Craig to E. S. Murphy, Unionist MP for Londonderry city, 18 Dec. 1936, PRONI, CAB 9B/13/3.

29. *The Tablet*, 19 Nov. 1932.

30. PRONI, CAB 9D/1/6.

31. *Ibid.*

32. M. Scott Moore to Blackmore, 27 Mar. 1926, *ibid.*, CAB 9R/57/1.

33. Ervine, 520—2, 532.

[134] 34. Notes on conference at Stormont Castle, 12 Dec. 1933, PRONI, CAB 9A/3/5.

35. Financial Diary, Mar.-Oct. 1938, manuscript note between pp. 122–3.

36. Ervine, 538.

Conclusion (pp. 123–5)

1. Ervine, 561.

Index